CHRISTIAN CLA

MW00790751

JOHN CALVIN

Sovereign Hope

6 studies
for individuals
or groups
with study notes

CLASSICS

Carolyn Nystrom

CAROLYN NYSTROM, Series Editor

IVP

InterVarsity Press
Downers Grove, Illinois

InterVarsity Press
P.O. Box 1400, Downers Grove, IL 60515-1426
World Wide Web: www.ivpress.com
E-mail: mail@ivpress.com

InterVarsity Press® is the book-publishing division of InterVarsity Christian Fellowship/USA®,
a student movement active on campus at hundreds of universities, colleges and schools of
nursing in the United States of America, and a member movement of the International
Fellowship of Evangelical Students. For information about local and regional activities, write
Public Relations Dept., InterVarsity Christian Fellowship/USA, 6400 Schroeder Rd., P.O. Box
7895, Madison, WI 53707-7895, or visit the IVCF website at <www.ivcf.org>.

All Scripture quotations, unless otherwise indicated, are taken from the Holy Bible, New
International Version®. NIV®. Copyright ©1973, 1978, 1984 by International Bible Society.
Used by permission of Zondervan Publishing House. All rights reserved.

Excerpts in studies 1, 2, 5 and 6 are taken from Calvin: Institutes of the Christian Religion
(Library of Christian Classics), edited by John T. McNeill. Used by permission of Westminster
John Knox Press.

Excerpt in study 3 is taken from Calvin's New Testament Commentaries: The Epistle of
Paul to the Romans and Thessalonians, David W. Torrance and Thomas F. Torrance, eds.,
R. Mackenzie, trans. (Grand Rapids, Mich.: Eerdmans, 1973), and used by permission.

Cover and interior illustrations: Roberta Polfus

ISBN 0-8308-2086-8

Printed in the United States of America ∞

P	18	17	16	15	14	13	12	11	10	9	8	7	6	5	4	3	2	1
Y	16	15	14	13	12	11	10	09	08	07	06	05	04	03	02			

CONTENTS

Introducing
John Calvin

He was loved. He was hated. But he was never ignored. John Calvin's enemies in Geneva, Switzerland, the city where he served as pastor, coined the slogan: "Better with Beza in hell than with Calvin in heaven." Calvin was accused of being harsh, inflexible, petty and cold. And there was much in his personality to support those claims.

At the same time Calvin's writings (some fifty-nine volumes) reflect a deep passion for God. His letters show loving concern and wise counsel to his friends and parishioners. When he married at age thirty-one, he loved and cared for the children of his previously widowed wife. When a friend died, he accepted guardianship of his friend's children as well. When his own death loomed near, he gave instructions for an unheralded burial in an unmarked pauper's grave. In spite of complaints against him, John Calvin lived the faith he taught.

Calvin's Impact

It's hard to overestimate John Calvin's influence on Protestant Christianity. Presbyterians, Baptists, various Reformed churches and many Anglican groups owe the shape of their theology to him. In the spiritual awakening of the eighteenth century in North America, Jonathan Edwards and George Whitefield each drew their preaching from the Calvinist theology of two centuries earlier.

We continue to see evidences of Calvin's heritage in most Protestant churches today. Do you hear the Scripture read aloud in your church—in your own language? Calvin was among the first to do this. Does the congregation sing (together) music based on Scripture? This too is a Calvin addition. Does your pastor preach from a passage of Scripture, explaining it verse by verse to the people? Another novelty promoted by Calvin. Does your church have officers such as elders and deacons? This kind of church government reflects John Calvin's understanding of Scripture. When your church celebrates the sacrament of communion, does the pastor review its meaning? Another Calvinism. Do you see three pieces of furniture at the front of your church sanctuary? In Calvin's churches a pulpit, a baptismal font and a communion table symbolized his definition of a church: a place where the Scripture is preached and the two sacraments taught by Christ are practiced. Do you believe that salvation comes by faith alone, based on Scripture alone, through the grace of Jesus Christ alone? Then you hold to the three *solas* of John Calvin and his colleagues of the Reformation.

Shaping the Child

Born in 1509 to Gerard and Jeanne Cauvin in Noyon in the Picardy region of France, John Calvin was about five years old when his mother died. His father remarried, adding two sisters to the existing family of three boys. In that era children were treated as small adults, with regular whippings to keep them in line. Disease plagued the villages so that every family knew death to both young and old. In a bad year whole neighborhoods could be wiped out in a few weeks.

Having raised his son in the teachings of the Roman Catholic Church, John's father decided that his most talented son should become a priest. So at the age of twelve John Calvin received the tonsure (symbolic haircut) of a cleric in the church and began its accompanying education. At the age of fourteen John (Jean in

French) entered the University of Paris, and studied the ancient languages, classical writers and early theologians. He was already persnickety by nature; his fellow Latin students dubbed him "The Accusative Case." But Calvin's study of Augustine (354-430) at that stage led him to rediscover many of the basic tenets of Christianity in the early church so that when he later developed a Protestant theology, readers find constant references to this early saint.

By the time Calvin reached the age of nineteen, his father decided that his son should leave his studies of theology and instead pursue a career in law. Calvin's father had quarreled with the local priest, but the decision was most likely financial. In an era without social services, it was important that sons enter a career likely to earn support for large segments of the extended family. So John left his priestly studies and went to Orleans to study law. His normal pattern had him eating little, studying until midnight and rising early to begin again. Not surprisingly, he became an excellent legal student—though he never practiced the trade. The combination of theological and classical education, along with legal training, is apparent throughout his later work as he structured an organized church around careful legal lines and wrote theology in patterns of terse logic.

Two important events happened during Calvin's legal education. His father died when John was twenty-two. By then John was committed to these studies—so he stayed with them. At that time he also began to experience the digestive upsets (perhaps from parasitic worms) that would affect him all of his life. Some biographers attribute his irritable disposition to constant nausea.

From Catholic to Protestant

By the age of twenty-three Calvin made a return visit to his studies of classical literature, publishing the first of many books, a commentary on the work of Roman philosopher Seneca. An even more important event happened during that same period—John Calvin became a Protestant. He writes little about it, mentions it only twice and does not even supply an exact date. But sometime between the ages of twenty-three and twenty-five, Calvin's general dissatisfaction with the loose morals of Catholic clergy and his intellectual attraction to the theology of Martin Luther and Ulrich Zwingli drew him across the great divide of the church into previously uncharted territory. His short comment in the introduction to his commentary on the Psalms reads, "God by sudden conversion subdued and brought my mind to a teachable frame." The Protestant church would never be the same. From that point on, Calvin's mark would mold its shape.

Predictably his relationship with the Catholic Church became tense. He was forced to leave Paris and go into seclusion in what he hoped would be the safety of his hometown in Noyon. Instead, he landed in jail "for uproar made in the church." When he was released, he moved to Basel and began what would become his greatest written work, *The Institutes of the Christian Religion.* He wrote the first edition, composed of six chapters, in 1536 when he was twenty-seven years old and prefaced the book with a twenty-page introduction to King Francis I of France. The purpose of his eloquent and respectful preface was to explain the new Protestant faith—prove that it was indeed Christian—and to beg the king to cease persecuting (and killing) those who chose it. Calvin's friend Beza later said of King Francis, "It could not have failed to win him from the error of his course—if only he had read it." During the course of Calvin's lifetime *The Institutes* (an outline and defense of the Reformed Christian faith) grew through five editions to eighty chapters spread over some fifteen hundred pages. In its various translations this work remains a basic textbook of Reformed theology for pastors, students and teachers of today.

Cursed to Geneva

What came next in Calvin's life was little less than a thunderbolt. God stationed him in Geneva—or perhaps his friend William Farel did so on God's behalf. It began in 1537 as a simple trip from Noyon to Strasbourg, where he planned to continue his writing and studies, but war blocked Calvin's intended route. So he traveled to Geneva, a city of some thirteen thousand, intending to spend the night and continue on his way. William Farel was in charge of a start-up Protestant church there and was facing tense confrontations among the newly converted Protestants and resident Catholics, along with general civil unrest. He *ordered* Calvin to stay with him in Geneva and help. Calvin, of course, declined. The conversation continued and intensified far into the night. In the end Farel uttered a curse against his friend: "I denounce unto you, in the name of Almighty God, that if, under the pretext of prosecuting your studies, you refuse to labor with us in this work of the Lord, the Lord will curse you, as seeking yourself rather than Christ." Both men saw this as the voice of God and Calvin stayed in Geneva.

Biographer Georgia Harkness describes the Geneva of 1536 as having "all the vices characteristic of a wealthy pleasure-loving medieval town. The influence of its priests and monks had not been morally wholesome. It had even been found necessary to set a special watch against the visits of 'the religious' to its red light district." Calvin's brand of "pure living and pure doctrine" was a shock. He lasted just short of three years before both he and Farel were ordered to leave Geneva—on three days' notice. In fairness to the city, Calvin had not been an easy guest. He had taken over civil laws to the extent of directing when people could use lights and how they were to choose their officials, and he had closed all businesses during the preaching of a sermon. He had refused to accept at the Communion table people who disagreed with him. And when his view of the Trinity was questioned, he refused to sign the Apostles', Nicene and Athanasian creeds, not because he disagreed with what these ancient creeds said but simply because he was ordered to do so. He exited Geneva and went to Strasbourg, where he stayed with his friend Martin Bucer, preached and taught theology.

Strasbourg and Marriage

In Strasbourg, Calvin developed a liturgy and form of worship that included unison confession, extemporaneous prayer and congregational singing, along with exegetical preaching from Scripture as the main focus of the service. All were new in his era, and they still form the basic outline of Sunday worship in Reformed churches. His *Strausbourg Psalter* contained hymns still sung, including "I Greet Thee Who My Sure Redeemer Art." Instead of a sacrament-centered worship (as the Catholic church had been) Calvin's worship became Word-centered (or sermon-centered), a distinction that remains today. Though hard at work, Calvin received little pay at Strasbourg and was often both cold and hungry.

On the personal side, at about the age of thirty Calvin began to search for a wife—in characteristic unromantic fashion. At one point he set a wedding date, having not yet chosen a bride, but had to cancel since no suitable woman emerged. At another point he made a tentative agreement with a young woman's family, then backed out when he heard someone question her character. Finally he settled on newly widowed Idelette de Bure, whom he married in August 1540 and grew to love—along with her two children.

In 1542 Idelette gave birth to their first (and only) child. During the process Calvin wrote to his friend Viret, "My brother, I will tell you what great fears I have as I write. My wife is going to give birth but not without grave danger, because her pregnancy is not yet full-term. May God protect us!" Jacques, their son, died shortly after birth. And Idelette, who had always been frail, never fully recovered. In the next few years Calvin wrote numerous notes to friends about her condition, detailing each small hope and improvement, but by 1547 he again wrote to Viret, "I fear something contrary to my hopes. . . . May God show favor toward us." Biographer Richard Stauffer writes, "Idelette died on March 29, 1549. Her husband helped her to the end. After assuring her that he would be an attentive father to the children whom she had had during her first marriage, he spoke to her about the grace of Christ, the transitoriness of this life, and the hope of eternal life. Then, stricken with sorrow, he stepped aside to pray before seeing her die peacefully."

Geneva for Life
Meanwhile, prior to Idelette's death, conditions in Geneva continued to deteriorate. Church leaders left—or were eliminated. The

civil government was in disarray. Intolerance prevailed on all sides. The city council voted to attempt to bring Calvin back. After a year of deliberation (nearly three and a half years after his exile) Calvin and Idelette reluctantly returned to Geneva in September of 1541. Calvin wrote that he did not want to be of "those who have more care for their own ease and profit than for the edification of the church." He was thirty-two. John Calvin lived and worked in Geneva, Switzerland, the rest of his life.

In spite of lacking both citizenship and voting rights in Geneva, Calvin shaped the environment there. He developed a church-centered community—sometimes far too diligently for the taste of ordinary citizens. He structured churches governed by officers. He served as pastor and teacher. He wrote commentaries for nearly every book of the Bible. (These commentaries remain standard references for pastors.) Since he preached several times a week, he wrote hundreds of sermons. His articles on various aspects of theology and church government still dot the shelves of libraries, church offices and like-minded laypersons.

God's Providence

Calvin's theology put God first. He believed that nothing happens without the "hidden will" of God. This resulted in what some term the "horrible decree" of predestination. Calvin did not originate this doctrine; he traced it to St. Augustine and ultimately to the apostle Paul. And though some find the thought that God chooses some people to be his own from the foundation of the world—and rejects others—abhorrent, Calvin took great comfort in the thought that no such momentous decision rests on mere humans. Indeed he believed that humans, being totally depraved by sin, did not have the ability to choose God. So God must do the choosing—and does so as a grand illustration of his grace.

John Calvin's work as a pastor, teacher, writer and theologian places him among the most influential people of the Protestant Reformation. When Calvin entered his fifties, his always-tenuous health began a steep decline. He died on May 27, 1564, at the age of fifty-five. At his own stern request he was buried in an unmarked grave without ceremony or song (though hundreds walked silently behind the casket to the site). What seems a strange burial for one who created worship services full of joy and song fit well with Calvin's theology. He wished that the glory of God should not be overshadowed by honoring people. "To God alone be glory."

How to Use a Christian Classics Bible Study
Christian Classics Bible studies are designed to introduce some of the key writers, preachers and teachers who have shaped our Christian thought over the centuries. Each guide has an introduction to the life and thought of a particular writer and six study sessions. The studies each have an introduction to the particular themes and writings in that study and the following components.

READ ——————————————————————————
This is an excerpt from the original writings.

GROUP DISCUSSION OR PERSONAL REFLECTION ————————
These questions are designed to help you explore the themes of the reading.

INTO THE WORD ——————————————————————
This includes a key Scripture to read and explore inductively. The text picks up on the themes of the study session.

ALONG THE ROAD ——————————————————————
These are ideas to carry you further and deeper into the themes of the study. Some can be used in a group session; many are for personal use and reflection.

The study notes at the end of the guide offer further helps and background on the study questions.

May these writings and studies enrich your life in Christ.

I

HOW CAN
WE KNOW GOD?
Luke 5:1-11

What are we made for? To know God.
What aim should we set ourselves in life? To know God. . . .
What is the best thing in life, bringing more joy, delight and contentment than anything else? Knowledge of God" (J. I. Packer, *Knowing God*).

John Calvin, in the opening paragraphs of his *Institutes*, starts his explanation of Christian theology by this basic principle: We must know God. And once we have caught even a glimpse of God, we will also know ourselves. That knowledge may prove uncomfortable. It may drive us to our knees. But it will give us a clear-eyed view of reality—and we will be the better for it.

 WITHOUT KNOWLEDGE OF SELF, THERE IS NO
KNOWLEDGE OF GOD

INSTITUTES OF THE CHRISTIAN RELIGION 1.1.1-3

Nearly all wisdom we possess, that is to say, true and sound wisdom, consists of two parts: the knowledge of God and of ourselves.

But, while joined by many bonds, which one precedes and brings forth the other is not easy to discern. In the first place, no one can look upon himself without immediately turning his thoughts to the contemplation of God, in whom he "lives and moves" [Acts 17:28]. For, quite clearly, the mighty gifts which we are endowed are hardly from ourselves; indeed, our very being is nothing but subsistence in the one God. Then by these benefits shed like dew from heaven upon us, we are led as by rivulets to the spring itself. . . .

[And] from the feeling of our own ignorance, vanity, poverty, infirmity, and—what is more—depravity and corruption, we recognize that the true light of wisdom, sound virtue, full abundance of every good, and purity of rightness rest in the Lord alone. To this extent we are prompted by our own ills to contemplate the good things of God; and we cannot seriously aspire to him before we begin to become displeased with ourselves. For what man in all the world would not gladly remain as he is—what man does not remain as he is—so long as he does not know himself, that is, while content with his own gifts, and either ignorant or unmindful of his own misery? Accordingly, the knowledge of ourselves not only arouses us to seek God, but also, as it were, leads us by the hand to find him.

Again, it is certain that man never achieves a clear knowledge of himself unless he has first looked upon God's face, and then descends from contemplating him to scrutinizing himself. For we always seem to ourselves righteous and upright and wise and holy—this pride is innate in all of us—unless by clear proofs we stand convinced of our own unrighteousness, foulness, folly, and impurity. Moreover, we are not thus convinced if we look merely to ourselves and not also to the Lord, who is the sole standard by which this judgment must be measured. . . .

Just so, an eye to which nothing is shown but black objects judges something dirty white or even rather darkly mottled to be whiteness itself. . . . As long as we do not look beyond the earth, being quite content with our own righteousness, wisdom, and virtue, we flatter ourselves most sweetly, and fancy ourselves all but demigods. Suppose we but once begin to raise our thoughts to God, and to ponder his nature, and how completely perfect are his right-eousness, wisdom, and power—the straightedge to which we must be shaped. Then, what masquerading earlier as righteousness was pleasing in us will soon grow filthy in its consummate wickedness. What wonderfully impressed us under the name of wisdom will stink in its very foolishness. What wore the face of power will prove itself the most miserable weakness. That is, what in us seems per-fection itself corresponds ill to the purity of God.

Hence that dread and wonder with which Scripture commonly represents the saints as stricken and overcome whenever they felt the presence of God.

 GROUP DISCUSSION OR PERSONAL REFLECTION ——

1. In the first paragraph above, John Calvin says that one way we can know God is to first look at ourselves and all the gifts God has given to us. What are some of the opportunities, experiences, personal qualities, skills or relationships that you see as God's gifts to you?

2. Calvin also says that we must "ponder [God's] nature, and how completely perfect are his righteousness, wisdom, and power— the straightedge to which we must be shaped." What do you find challenging about this?

 INTO THE WORD————————————————————

3. *Read Luke 5:1-11.* Put yourself in this story as one of the characters. Tell the story as seen through the eyes of the character you have chosen.

4. What does your character know about Jesus as a result of this event?

What does your character know about himself?

5. What are some of the ways that Jesus helped Peter to know him (vv. 1-7)?

6. Notice Peter's words in verse 8. Why did he respond in this way to what looked like a successful fishing trip?

7. Why is fear such a frequent response to a clear view of God?

8. Why do you think Jesus began his response to Peter with the words, "Don't be afraid?"

9. How did Peter's glimpse of Jesus and himself through the events of this story begin to equip him for the challenge of verse 10?

10. John Calvin wrote in the segment quoted above, "We cannot seriously aspire to [God] before we begin to become displeased with ourselves." How have you seen this to be true of your own experience with God?

11. Much of today's culture tells us that we ought to "feel good about ourselves." In view of Peter's (and Calvin's) experience, how would you respond to this cultural value?

12. What are some ways that you can rightly know yourself—and God?

 ALONG THE ROAD ————————————————————————

📖 Place yourself in a setting where some aspect of God's creation helps you to focus on his greatness. This could be as simple as studying the formation of petals on a flower or the striations of tree bark or the texture of a rock. Or it could be as huge as a starry night, a sunrise or the expanse of ocean shore. Silently meditate on what you hear, see, touch, taste and smell—how all of this reminds you of God. Make journal notes on what you see of God's character in this object of his creation. Then worship him in prayer. If you are in a group, separate from each other while you do this exercise, then come back together and discuss what you have discovered.

📖 Take a look at your own heart. What are some ways that you protect yourself from seeing your own flaws? Ask God to graciously reveal some of these faults (and perhaps sins) to you. Confess these to God, receiving his forgiveness. Expect (and welcome) that this view of yourself will increase your need of him.

📖 Sing or read the hymn "How Great Thou Art." Pause after each verse for brief sentences of prayer based on that verse.

How Great Thou Art

O Lord my God! When I in awesome wonder
Consider all the worlds Thy hands have made,
I see the stars, I hear the rolling thunder,
Thy power thro'out the universe displayed.

Refrain:
Then sings my soul, my Savior God, to Thee:
How great Thou art! How great Thou art!
Then sings my soul, my Savior God, to Thee:
How great thou art! How great thou art!

When thro' the woods and forest glades I wander
And hear the birds sing sweetly in the trees,
When I look down from lofty mountain grandeur,
And hear the brook and feel the gentle breeze;

Refrain

And when I think that God, His Son not sparing,
Sent Him to die, I scarce can take it in;
That on the cross, my burden gladly bearing,
He bled and died to take away my sin.

Refrain

When Christ shall come with shout of acclamation
And take me home, what joy shall fill my heart!
Then I shall bow in humble adoration,
And there proclaim, my God, how great Thou art!

Refrain

STUART K. HINE, 1953*

II

IF GOD'S GONNA DO
WHAT GOD'S GONNA DO,
WHY PRAY?

1 Kings 18:16-46

*D*o you ever wonder if prayer is just an exercise in talking to yourself? And if God *is* indeed listening, why would an almighty God (who can do anything he wants) listen to your prayers? Your reasoning might go something like this: Why should I talk to God anyway? God already knows what I need; it even says so in Scripture. And if God designed the universe and controls all that happens in it, how could I expect my prayers to make any difference? Isn't prayer presumptuous, as if my puny human mind could remind God of something he hasn't already thought of? Why should I ask anything of God? God will do whatever he chooses anyway. Right?

Among Reformation theologians John Calvin had one of the strongest views of God's providence. He believed that God designs all things at all times. Nothing escapes his care. With that concept of God we might expect that Calvin would ask the same questions we ask in our moments of doubt about prayer. Yet he wrote one of the most beautiful pictures of prayer in Christian literature. Calvin (along with Scripture) instructs us to pray—but perhaps for different reasons than we might expect.

 ON PRAYER ─────────────────────────

INSTITUTES OF THE CHRISTIAN RELIGION 3.20.2-3

It is . . . by the benefit of prayer that we reach those riches which are laid up for us with the Heavenly Father. For there is a communion of men with God by which, having entered the heavenly sanctuary, they appeal to him in person concerning his promises in order to experience, where necessity so demands, that what they believed was not vain, although he had promised it in word alone. Therefore we see that to us nothing is promised to be expected from the Lord, which we are not also bidden to ask of him in prayers. So true is it that we dig up by prayer the treasures that were pointed out by the Lord's gospel, and which our faith has gazed upon.

Words fail to explain how necessary prayer is, and in how many ways the exercise of prayer is profitable. Surely, with good reason the Heavenly Father affirms that the only stronghold of safety is in calling upon his name [cf. Joel 2:32]. By so doing we invoke the presence both of his providence, through which he sustains us, weak as we are and well-nigh overcome, and of his goodness, through which he receives us, miserably burdened with sins, unto grace; and, in short, it is by prayer that we call him to reveal himself as wholly present to us. Hence comes an extraordinary peace and repose to our consciences. For having disclosed to the Lord the necessity that was pressing upon us, we even rest fully in the thought that none of our ills is hid from him who, we are convinced, has both the will and the power to take the best care of us. . . .

The Lord instructed his people to pray, for he ordained it not so much for his own sake as for ours. . . . First, that our hearts may be fired with a zealous and burning desire ever to seek, love, and serve him, while we become accustomed in every need to flee to him as a sacred anchor. Secondly, that there may enter our hearts no desire and no wish at all of which we should be ashamed to make him a witness, while we learn to set all our wishes before his eyes, and even to pour out our whole hearts. Thirdly, that we be prepared to receive his benefits with true gratitude of heart and thanksgiving, benefits that our prayer reminds us come from his hand [cf. Ps. 145:15-16]. Fourthly, moreover that, having obtained what we were seeking, and being convinced that he has answered our prayers, we should be led to meditate upon his kindness more ardently. And fifthly, that at the same time we embrace with greater delight those things which we acknowledge to have been obtained by prayers. Finally, that use and experience may, according to the measure of our feebleness, confirm his providence, while we understand not only that he promises never to fail us, and of his own will opens the way to call upon him at the very point of necessity, but also that he ever extends his hand to help his own, not wet-nursing them with words but defending them with present help. . . .

"For the eyes of the Lord are upon the righteous, and his ears toward their prayers" [I Peter 3:12; Ps. 34:15].

 GROUP DISCUSSION OR PERSONAL REFLECTION ——

1. Why do you pray (or not pray)?

2. In the first paragraph John Calvin speaks of prayer as "a communion of men with God by which, having entered the heavenly sanctuary, they appeal to him in person." Imagine for a moment that you live in a world where prayer has not yet been discovered— and you come upon this quote. What would you do, think, feel or wonder?

3. John Calvin begins the last paragraph above by saying that

God tells us to pray "not so much for his own sake as for ours." Then he lists six benefits of prayer. Which of these have you experienced recently? How?

Which would you like to develop more fully? Why?

 INTO THE WORD────────────────────────────

4. *Read 1 Kings 18:16-46.* If you were to portray this story visually, what are some of the images you would try to capture?

5. It had not rained in Israel for more than three years. What do verses 16-20 suggest about why that might be?

6. Elijah challenged his people: "How long will you waver between two opinions? If the LORD is God, follow him; but if Baal is

God, follow him" (v. 21). What did Elijah do that would make the results of his challenge obvious (vv. 22-34)?

7. Study Elijah's prayer of verses 36-37, noticing especially the words *you* and *your.* How does this brief prayer illustrate worship, respect and faith?

8. Reread verses 38-39. Most of us have not experienced anything as dramatic as fire from heaven. But God reveals himself to us in other more quiet ways. What experience of your own has caused you to say or think, "The Lord—he is God"?

9. *Read 1 Kings 18:1-2.* As you review verses 41-45, what further communication do you sense between God and Elijah?

10. When have you had to wait for God's response to your prayers?

What have you learned about yourself and about God during that time?

11. Look again at the questioning title of this chapter, "If God's gonna do what God's gonna do, why pray?" In view of Calvin's writing, Elijah's story and your own experience, how would you answer that question?

 ALONG THE ROAD ——————————————

✐ John Calvin believed that "all things happen by God's plan, that nothing takes place by chance" (*Institutes* 1.17.6). Yet God invites us to pray, participating in some mysterious way in the work that he has already designed. Pray, asking God to show you what place he has designed for you in the work of prayer. As much as you are able, submit your own wants to his grand plan.

✐ When God answered Elijah's prayer, the people of Israel "fell prostrate and cried, 'The LORD—he is God! The LORD—he is God!'" In prayer, express your own worship of God as Lord of all things and all events—including yourself. Use a body position that helps you express this worship.

✐ "The eyes of the LORD are on the righteous and his ears are attentive to their cry" (Psalm 34:15). Carry this quotation with you for the next few days as a reminder that our compassionate God is constantly present with you and constantly inviting you to prayer.

⚋ Prayerfully read or sing the hymn "Whate'er My God Ordains Is Right" by Samuel Rodigast. If you come to a phrase that speaks particularly about your own current situation, pause and talk to God about it.

Whate'er My God Ordains Is Right

Whate'er my God ordains is right:
his holy will abideth;
I will be still whate'er he doth,
and follow where he guideth.
He is my God: though dark my road,
he holds me that I shall not fall:
wherefore to him I leave it all.

Whate'er my God ordains is right:
he never will deceive me;
he leads me by the proper path;
I know he will not leave me.
I take, content, what he hath sent;
his hand can turn my griefs away,
and patiently I wait his day.

Whate'er my God ordains is right:
though now this cup, in drinking,
may bitter seem to my faint heart,
I take it, all unshrinking.
My God is true; each morn anew
sweet comfort yet shall fill my heart,
and pain and sorrow shall depart.

Whate'er my God ordains is right:
here shall my stand be taken;
though sorrow, need, or death be mine,
yet am I not forsaken.
My Father's care is round me there;
he holds me that I shall not fall:
and so to him I leave it all.

SAMUEL RODIGAST, 1676
TRANS. CATHERINE WINKWORTH, 1863

III

WHAT DOES IT MEAN TO BE CHOSEN BY GOD?

Romans 8:28-39

*T*wo brothers grew up in the same home, graduated from the same schools and attended the same church. One became a devout, lifelong Christian. The other didn't. Why? It is a mystery to most Christians. John Calvin wondered about the same thing. Why did some people seem to have no interest at all in what he saw as good news from God?

Calvin was a thorough student. He studied the fifteen hundred years of Christian theologians. He analyzed Scripture phrase by phrase and came to the conclusion that we are asking the wrong question. The question is not *why,* but *who.* Who is in charge of people coming to God? God himself is—through his own work of predestination. *Predestination* is a term linked irrevocably to John Calvin. But it came to him through Augustine—and the apostle Paul. What follows are some of Calvin's comments on predestination drawn from parts of his commentary on Romans.

 CALLED BY GOD

CALVIN'S NEW TESTAMENT COMMENTARIES
Even to them that are called according to his purpose. . . . Believers, Paul says, do not acquire godliness by their own efforts, but are

rather led by the hand of God, since He has chosen them to be his peculiar people.

For whom he foreknew, he also foreordained. . . . The verb . . . translated *predestinate,* refers to the circumstances of the present passage. Paul meant only that God had determined that all whom He has adopted should bear the image of Christ. . . . No one can be an heir of heaven who has not first been conformed to the only-begotten Son of God. . . .

And whom He foreordained, them He also called. . . . By teaching us that they are now *called,* Paul means that God does not conceal what He has determined to do with them, but has disclosed it, in order that they may bear with equanimity and patience the condition laid upon them. *Calling* . . . has the power of the Spirit connected with it, for Paul is dealing with the elect whom God not only constrains by His spoken Word, but also draws inwardly.

Justification might quite well be extended to include the continuation of the divine favour from the time of the calling of the believer to his death. . . .

Paul adds that those who are now oppressed by the cross shall be *glorified,* so that their troubles and reproaches are not to bring them any loss.

What then shall we say? Having sufficiently proved his point, Paul now breaks into a series of exclamations, by which he expresses the greatness of soul which believers ought to possess while adversity urges them to despair. He teaches us by these words that the invincible courage which overcomes all temptations resides in the fatherly favour of God.

If God is for us, who is against us? . . . There is no power under heaven or above it which can resist the arm of God. If, therefore, we have Him as our defender, we need fear no harm whatever. . . . Believers are certainly often shaken, but are never utterly cast down. In short, the apostle's object was to show that the godly soul ought to stand on the inward testimony of the Holy Spirit, and not to depend on external things.

He that spared not His own Son. . . . This passage ought to admonish and arouse us to consider what Christ brings to us with Himself, for as He is a pledge of God's boundless love towards us, so He has not been sent to us void of blessings or empty-handed, but filled with all heavenly treasures, so that those who possess Him may not want anything that is necessary for their complete happiness. . . .

Who shall lay anything to the charge of God's elect? We must, however, note here that according to Paul, to be *justified* means simply to be accounted just by having been absolved from the sentence of God. . . . The devil, to be sure, accuses all the godly; and the law of God itself and their own conscience also reprove them. But none of these have any influence upon the judge who justifies them. No adversary, therefore, can shake, much less destroy, our salvation. . . .

Who is he that shall condemn? As no one can succeed in his accusation when the judge absolves, so there remains no condemnation, when the laws have been satisfied and the penalty already paid. . . .

Paul adds still more—Christ, he states, now sits at the right hand of the Father. . . . This great security which dares to triumph over the devil, death, sin and the gates of hell, ought to be deeply implanted in all godly hearts, for our faith is nothing, unless we are persuaded for certain that Christ is ours. . . .

Who maketh intercession for us. . . . Christ holds all things in subjection under His feet from His lofty throne, Paul represents Him as a Mediator, whose presence it would be absurd for us to dread, since He not only invites us to Himself in a kindly manner, but also appears for us before the Father as Intercessor. . . .

Who shall separate us from the love of Christ? . . . The meaning of the words is that whatever may happen, we must stand firm in the belief that God, who once in His love embraced us, never ceases to care for us. . . . Indeed, our faith should be borne up on wings by the promises of God, and penetrate to heaven through all the intervening obstacles. . . .

Shall tribulation, or anguish, or persecution? . . . These three temptations differ in this way—tribulation included every kind of trouble or loss, but *anguish* is the inward feeling, when difficulties reduce us to not knowing what course to follow. . . . *Persecution* properly denotes the tyrannical violence by which the children of God are undeservedly tormented by the ungodly. . . .

Even as it is written. . . . Paul hints that the terror of death is so far from being a reason for our falling away, that it is almost always the lot of the servants of God to have death in front of their eyes. . . . To say that they *are killed all the day long* means that death threatens them in such a way that there is little difference between such a life and death.

We are more than conquerors. . . . It sometimes happens that believers seem to have been overcome and to be bowed down in utter weariness. . . . The assurance of this, fixed deep in our hearts, will always draw us from hell to the light of life, and will be of sufficient strength to support us.

For I am persuaded, that neither death, nor life. . . . We are not to fear that our faith in our adoption will be destroyed by the continuance of evils, however long it may be. . . .

We are to have confidence that He who has begun a good work in us, will accomplish it until the day of the Lord Jesus.

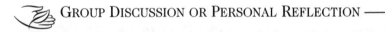 GROUP DISCUSSION OR PERSONAL REFLECTION ———

1. From your own perspective, what has drawn (or is drawing) you toward Christ?

2. Have you found that hardship has strengthened or weakened your faith? Explain.

INTO THE WORD————————————————————

3. *Read Romans 8:28-39.* What do you see here that you appreciate?

4. If you were going through difficult circumstances, what would you find encouraging about verses 28-30?

5. Using the biblical text along with Calvin's notes, how would you define the terms *foreknew, predestined, called, justified, conformed* and *glorified* (vv. 28-30)?

6. According to this progression, how does our salvation begin, how does it end, and what happens in between?

7. What power and work does Paul ascribe to Jesus (vv. 31-34)?

8. If you were worried about whether you could keep on in your Christian faith, what do you see in these verses that would encourage you?

9. Reread aloud verses 35-39. What is the emotional impact of God's love described in this way?

10. Of verse 35, Calvin writes, "We must stand firm in the belief that God, who once in his love embraced us, never ceases to care for us." What are some ways that you would like to respond to that kind of love?

11. Are there people you know who appear to have fallen away from their faith in Jesus? In view of this passage of Scripture, how can you be praying for them?

12. Calvin believed that no one deserved God's love and that no one could turn to God by their own efforts. What astounded him was that God did, in fact, choose some—from the beginning of time.

God showered his love on these people, called them to faith and granted them the free gift of salvation. In view of this section of Romans 8, what are your thoughts on that subject?

13. We mere mortals have no way of knowing whom God has called as his own. We must assume that everyone we touch is included in his love—and extend that offer to them. It is God's Spirit who will create a response. How can you begin to express that love to someone you would like to see come to faith in Jesus?

 ALONG THE ROAD ──────────────────────────

◲ One of the steps toward glorification that Paul outlines in Romans 8:28-30 is that we are being "conformed to the likeness of his Son." This echoes the way God created humans in the beginning. Prayerfully read of that creation in Genesis 1:26-27 and Genesis 2:7. Meditate on what it means to be molded by God in his image, to have the breath of God breathed into you. After a time of silent meditation express in prayer your desire for God to continue shaping your character to become more and more like Jesus.

◲ We humans cannot know who God will draw to himself, so we can rightly pray for *anyone* to come into his family. Spend time praying for several people you would most like to see come to saving faith. Then add one person who seems unlikely to respond to Jesus—and focus on prayer for that person. (No one is beyond the power of God's love!)

Look again at your response to question one under "Group Discussion or Personal Reflection." Try, with a little sanctified imagination, to picture what your salvation story might have looked like from God's point of view. Thank God for what you see.

Sing or read "I Sought the Lord" (1904) as your own prayer of thanks to God—who loves you.

I Sought the Lord

I sought the Lord, and afterward I knew
He moved my soul to seek him, seeking me;
It was not I that found, O Saviour true,
No, I was found of thee.

Thou didst reach forth thy hand and mine enfold;
I walked and sank not on the storm-vexed sea,—
'Twas not so much that I on thee took hold,
As thou, dear Lord, on me.

I find, I walk, I love, but, O the whole
Of love is but my answer, Lord, to thee;
For thou wert long beforehand with my soul,
always thou lovedst me.

ANONYMOUS, C. 1904

IV

HOW DO I
FACE DEATH?

2 Corinthians 4:6—5:1

We spend more time getting ready for two weeks away
from work than we will for our last two weeks on earth," writes
John Cloud in *Time* magazine's feature article about dying (September 18, 2000). We make our plans as if we will live forever.
And when death comes, even Christians have the sense that God
has somehow failed us. Or conversely, we deny the pain of death
and smile through gritted teeth.

But death came soon, often and unexpectedly in Calvin's era. It
wouldn't take much: an accident with a horse, a sudden fever, an
unpopular religious or political statement. John Calvin lived to
the age of fifty-five. By that age the normal person of his day
would suffer constant physical pain and have witnessed the
deaths of numerous friends and family members. For them, preparing for death was a part of life. It was a time to write letters,
give advice, say goodbye to friends, reflect on the value of your
life, distribute your belongings—and pray.

John Calvin wrote numerous letters. In his early life many of
his letters were words of encouragement and comfort to friends
who were near death. Near the end his letters were his own fare-
wells. We can learn much about the state of Calvin's soul (not to

mention his body) as we read his mail—and perhaps better prepare ourselves for a healthy look at an event that comes to us all. And, after that, we can look even further—to living past the end.

READING CALVIN'S MAIL

The first letter was written to five friends in Lyons facing execution.

Geneva, 15 May 1553
My very dear Brothers:
. . . The King has peremptorily refused all the requests made by Messieurs of Berne, as you will see by the copies of the letters, so nothing further is to be looked for from that quarter. Nay, wherever we look here below, God has stopped the way. . . . Now, at this present hour, necessity itself exhorts you more than ever to turn your whole mind heavenward. As yet, we know not what will be the event. But since it appears as though God would use your blood to sign His truth, there is nothing better than for you to prepare yourselves to that end, beseeching Him so to subdue you to His good pleasure, that nothing may hinder you from following whithersoever he shall call. . . . You shall not faint under the load of temptations, however heavy it be, any more than he did who won so glorious a victory, that in the midst of our miseries it is an unfailing pledge of our triumph. Since it pleases Him to employ you to the death in maintaining His quarrel, He will strengthen your hands in the fight, and will not suffer a single drop of your blood to be spent in vain. . . .

The five men who received this letter were soon burned at the stake for their faith. They sang psalms and quoted Scripture to each other until the end.

Geneva, 27 August 1561
To Theodore Beza:
I am obliged to dictate this letter to you from bed, and in the deepest affliction from the loss of my dear friend De Varennes, who has hitherto been my principal stay and comfort in all my troubles. One thing affords me no slight consolation in my sorrow, which is that nothing could have been more calm than the manner of his death,

which he seemed to invite with out-stretched arms as cheerfully as if it had been some delicious enjoyment. . . .

A week later, Calvin was again writing to his friend Beza with more sad news.

Geneva, 3 September 1561
To Theodore Beza:
Lest I should have to mourn but for one death, three days after that of my friend De Varennes, the oldest pastor has followed him to the tomb. We have given up all of hopes respecting the life of Baduel. Yesterday the wife of our treasurer, after having seemed recovered from the sufferings of childbirth, died suddenly of convulsions of the nerves. . . . And not to go on enumerating our losses, Nicholas Ingee was suffocated by a catarrh in the short space of nine hours. . . .

By July of 1563 Calvin was dealing with personal suffering from a disease that would kill him a year later. He wrote to a friend about the spiritual blessings of suffering.

Geneva, 5 August 1563
To Madame DeColigny:
I thank God who has put you in the way of recovery from an illness which we had great reason to fear might have been mortal. . . . You know Madam, how we should turn to our profit both the chastisements we receive from the hand of our merciful Father and the succour which he send [sic] in time of need. It is certain that all diseases ought not only to humble us in setting before our eyes our frailty, but also cause us to look into ourselves, that having recognized our own poverty we may place all our trust in his mercy. They should, moreover, serve us for medicines to purge us from worldly affections, and retrench what is superfluous in us, and since they are to us the messengers of death, we ought to learn to have one foot raised to take our departure when it shall please God. Nevertheless, he lets us taste of his bounty as often as he delivers us from them. . . .

In February 1564, Calvin wrote to the physicians of Montpellier describing his illnesses, which included arthritic pains, stone or the gravel (kidney stones?), cholic, hemorrhoids, expectoration of blood, gaurtan ague (high fever), an ulcer in the hemorrhoid veins, intestinal ascardes (worms), gout in the feet, and phlegmlike paste in his stomach. He was no longer able to ride horseback or walk more than a few yards. His next letters would be from his deathbed. Calvin's last known letter was to his friend Farel.

> Geneva, 2 May 1564
> To Farel:
> Farewell, my most excellent and upright brother; and since it is the will of God that you should survive me in the world, live mindful of our intimacy, which, as it was useful to the church of God, so the fruits of it await us in heaven. I am unwilling that you should fatigue yourself for my sake. I draw my breath with difficulty, and every moment I am in expectation of breathing my last. It is enough that I live and die for Christ, who is to all his followers a gain both in life and death. Again I bid you and your brethren Farewell.

John Calvin died in Geneva May 27, 1564.

 GROUP DISCUSSION OR PERSONAL REFLECTION ——

1. We don't often have the opportunity to read someone else's mail. What do you find interesting about John Calvin's letters?

2. What do you find of value in Calvin's approach to death?

3. Take a second look at Calvin's letter to Madame DeColigny. What would you want to put to use here if Calvin had written this letter to you?

 INTO THE WORD ─────────────────────────────────

4. *Read 2 Corinthians 4:6—5:1.* Paul says in verse 6 that God has given us "the light of the knowledge of the glory of God in the face of Christ." But he opens by saying that we carry this treasure in jars of clay. What combinations of treasure and clay do you see in 4:7-10?

5. What reminders have you had recently that the human body is as fragile as a clay jar?

6. Paul mentions the "spirit of faith" in 4:13. How does his Christian faith help him to deal with the fragility of life (4:13-15)?

7. Paul says in 4:16 that "we [Christians] do not lose heart." Why (4:16—5:1)?

8. In 4:17 Paul speaks of "light and momentary troubles." If he were speaking about your life, what troubles would he be describing?

How can you approach those troubles in a way that points toward eternal glory?

9. How is a tent (5:1) also a good symbol for our bodies?

10. Quickly review the entire passage. What reasons for joy do you find here?

11. In 2 Corinthians 5:1 we read that God is building an "eternal house in heaven" for us. How has God begun to prepare you for that?

 ALONG THE ROAD

✍ Many of us have an inner sense of "home." Perhaps this is a special place in your own home, or a place you once visited, or an imagined place you have never seen but always longed for. Close your eyes and mentally bring yourself to that place that is "home" to you. Heaven is all of that—and more.

Perhaps God gives us a sense of longing for home as part of our personal preparation for heaven. Read 2 Corinthians 5:1-5 and thank God for all that you find there.

✍ According to this passage God has created his people as eternal beings. We live here for a while in temporary housing: bodies as fragile as a clay jar or a tent. But this era of "camping out" prepares us for eternity—living past the end. Create a timeline, marking the beginning with your birth date. Create marks along the way recording significant events that have helped prepare you for eternity. Mark your death (date unknown), but then extend the timeline on beyond that mark. Create appropriate symbols there that cause you to look forward with joy to that eternal section of your time line.

❧ The hymn "I Greet Thee, Who My Sure Redeemer Art" helps us to look forward to heaven, not only for what we will have there, but also for whom we will be with. This hymn was published in the *Strausbourg Psalter* in 1545 under John Calvin's leadership. Many think that Calvin composed the words himself. Read this hymn as a prayer that helps you to bridge from this life to the next. Pause at the end of each verse to speak personally to God about the subjects raised in that verse.

I Greet Thee, Who My Sure Redeemer Art

I greet thee, who my sure Redeemer art,
my only trust and Savior of my heart,
who pain didst undergo for my poor sake;
I pray thee from our hearts all cares to take.

Thou art the King of mercy and of grace,
reigning omnipotent in ev'ry place:
so come, O King, and our whole being sway;
shine on us with the light of thy pure day.

Thou art the Life, by which alone we live,
and all our substance and our strength receive;
O comfort us in death's approaching hour,
strong-hearted then to face it by thy pow'r.

Thou hast the true and perfect gentleness,
no harshness hast thou and no bitterness:
make us to taste the sweet grace found in thee
and ever stay in thy sweet unity.

Our hope is in no other save in thee;
our faith is built upon thy promise free;
O grant to us such stronger hope and sure
That we can boldly conquer and endure.

STRAUSBOURG PSALTER, 1545
TRANS. ELIZABETH L. SMITH, 1868

V

WHAT IS THE CHURCH ALL ABOUT?

Ephesians 2:11-22

*T*he churches in my life have been few but important. My childhood was spent in a small Pilgrim Holiness church in rural southern Ohio where I heard the gospel preached by a husband and wife team who shared the ministry. During a revival at that church I walked to the front, knelt at the altar, asked Jesus to come into my heart and was later baptized in a nearby creek. There I experienced the exuberance of rural camp meetings and learned not to be afraid of such expressions of spiritual fervor. That church had its shortcomings: it was far too strict about things like clothing and recreational activities, and some of the emotional fervor was excessive. But that church introduced me to Jesus. And I have been thankful ever since.

When I was a teen, my family became Baptist—and we attended a small church in a nearby town. These people were serious about the Bible! They carried their King James Scofield version everywhere. (Mine was red.) They marked it and quoted it and argued over the minutiae of texts. And they let just about anybody do the work of the church. When they needed someone to lead the Christmas play, I put it together—at the age of sixteen—and had the pastor kneeling as a wise man. (My own private joke.) And when they ran short of musicians, I practiced three hours a day so I could pound out gospel songs on their piano on Sunday morning. That church, too, had its shortcomings. For all of the study of Scripture, the people had little knowledge of Christian beliefs—apart from their own. And their arguments led to bickering and unkindness toward each other. But I learned to love the Bible there. And I learned to enjoy doing the work of the church.

As an adult I became a suburban Presbyterian and am one of the few people I know who have been in the same church all of their adult lives. There I have learned a reasoned, thoughtful faith, one that worships God with quiet reverence and skillful music and liturgy begun by Christians hundreds of years ago. With several decades of longevity I have served God and his people in almost every imaginable way: preschool aide, ceiling tile installer, elder and even interim minister. This church too has its flaws (which I choose not to name). But this church has molded me as a Christian in ways that make me constantly thankful. Three churches—each quite different. But as I think over my life in the church, I mirror the words of Psalm 52:8: "I am like an olive tree flourishing in the house of God."

 ## THE MARKS OF THE CHURCH

INSTITUTES OF THE CHRISTIAN RELIGION 4.1.7-9

Holy Scripture speaks of the church in two ways. Sometimes by the term "church" it means that which is actually in God's presence, into which no persons are received but those who are children of God by grace of adoption and true members of Christ by sanctification of the Holy Spirit. Then, indeed, the church includes not only the saints presently living on earth, but all the elect from the beginning of the world. Often, however, the name "church" designates the whole multitude of men, spread over the earth who profess to worship one God and Christ. By baptism we are initiated into faith in him; by partaking in the Lord's Supper we attest our unity in true doctrine and love; in the Word of the Lord we have agreement, and for the preaching of the Word the ministry instituted by Christ is preserved. In this church are mingled many hypocrites who have nothing of Christ but the name and outward appearance. There are very many ambitious, greedy, envious persons, evil speakers and some of quite unclean life. Such are tolerated for a time either because they cannot be convicted by a competent tribunal or because a vigorous discipline does not always flourish as it ought.

Just as we may believe, therefore, that the former church invisible to us, is visible to the eyes of God alone, so we are commanded to revere and keep communion with the latter, which is called "church" in respect to men. . . .

Therefore, according to God's secret predestination (as Augustine says), "many sheep are without, and many wolves are within." . . .

Because he foresaw it to be of some value for us to know who were to be counted as his children, he has in this regard accommodated himself to our capacity. And, since assurance of faith was not necessary, he substituted for it a certain charitable judgment whereby we recognize as members of the church those who, by confession of faith, by example of life, and by partaking of the sacraments, profess the same God and Christ with us.

He has, moreover, set off by plainer marks the knowledge of his very body to us, knowing how necessary it is to our salvation. . . .

From this the face of the church comes forth and becomes visible to our eyes. Wherever we see the Word of God purely preached and heard, and the sacraments administered according to Christ's institution, there, it is not to be doubted, a church of God exists [cf. Eph. 2:20]. For this promise cannot fail: "Wherever two or three are gathered in my name, there I am in the midst of them: [Matt. 18:20].

But that we may clearly grasp the sum of this matter, we must proceed by the following steps: the church universal is a multitude gathered from all nations; it is divided and dispersed in separate places, but agrees on the one truth of divine doctrine, and is bound by the bond of the same religion. . . .

If it has the ministry of the Word and honors it, if it has the administration of the sacraments, it deserves without doubt to be held and considered a church. For it is certain that such things are not without fruit. In this way we preserve for the universal church its unity, which devilish spirits have always tried to sunder; and we do not defraud of their authority those lawful assemblies which have been set up in accordance with local needs. . . .

The Lord esteems the communion of his church so highly that he counts as a traitor and apostate from Christianity anyone who arrogantly leaves any Christian society, provided it cherishes the true ministry of Word and sacraments. He so esteems the authority of the church that when it is violated he believes his own diminished. . . .

It is also no common praise to say that Christ has chosen and set apart the church as his bride, "without spot or wrinkle" [Eph. 5:27], "his body and . . . fullness" [Eph. 1:23]. From this it follows that separation from the church is the denial of God and Christ. Hence, we must even more avoid so wicked a separation. For when with all our might we are attempting the overthrow of God's truth, we deserve to have him hurl the whole thunderbolt of his wrath to crush us. Nor can any more atrocious crime be conceived than for us by sacrilegious disloyalty to violate the marriage that the only-begotten Son of God deigned to contract with us.

 GROUP DISCUSSION OR PERSONAL REFLECTION ———

1. What has been one of your best experiences with church?

2. What was one of your worst experiences with church?

3. Calvin says that a true church is one where "we see the Word of God purely preached and heard, and the sacraments administered according to Christ's institution." What do you appreciate about this definition?

 INTO THE WORD

4. *Read Ephesians 2:11-22.* What words, phrases and concepts here help to define church?

5. What is missing from the lives of those who are left out of the body of Christ (vv. 11-12)?

6. What changes does Christ bring to those who are "without God in the world" (vv. 13-18)?

7. How, according to verses 13-18, does Jesus impact the way God's people relate to each other?

8. If you were to use verses 13-18 as the basis of prayer for your church or fellowship group, what would you ask God for?

9. What is church—according to verses 19-22?

10. What contrasts do you see between the person living in the situation described in verses 11-12 and the person living in the situation described in verses 19-22?

11. Why might you want to be part of the church as it is described here?

12. In what areas would you like to see your church become more like what is described in this text?

13. What part can you play in the structure described in verses 19-22?

 ALONG THE ROAD ————————————————

This week do a church tour of your town or community. Sit quietly in several sanctuaries praying for the well-being of this particular church—and for God's grace to work in and through the people there. For churches that you are unable to enter, walk around the outside of the building praying for God's power to be at work there.

Worship in a service different from your own. Look for evidences of God's work among the people of that congregation.

✐ Create a timeline of your own history of churches—each church that has played a significant role in your life. Note significant memories and events that relate to your spiritual growth.

Pray, thanking God for these churches and the people there who have influenced you for good.

✐ Calvin says, "The church includes not only the saints presently living on earth, but all the elect from the beginning of the world." Page through a book of church history, beginning with the year one. Stop occasionally to note a particular event or person who has shaped the course of Christian faith—and thank God.

✐ Practice the discipline of forgiveness. Calvin quotes Augustine in admitting that there are many "wolves" within the Christian church. In prayer, bring some of your painful church experiences to God—and begin to forgive.

✐ Page through a hymnal and find the earliest hymn in the book. (Many hymnals have date indexes in the back.) Bring to mind the Christians who first sang this hymn: their culture, language, circumstances and faith. Then read or sing the hymn, recognizing your own connection with them across the centuries. You might want to try the following 1866 hymn by Samuel J. Stone.

The Church's One Foundation

The church's one foundation is Jesus Christ, her Lord;
She is his new creation by water and the Word;
From heav'n he came and sought her to be his holy bride;
With his own blood he bought her, and for her life he died.

Elect from ev'ry nation, yet one o'er all the earth,
Her charter of salvation one Lord, one faith, one birth;
One holy name she blesses, partakes one holy food,
And to one hope she presses, with ev'ry grace endued.

Though with a scornful wonder men see her sore oppressed,
By schisms rent asunder, by heresies distressed,
Yet saints their watch are keeping, their cry goes up, "How long?"
And soon the night of weeping shall be the morn of song.

The church shall never perish! Her dear Lord to defend,
To guide, sustain, and cherish, is with her to the end;
Though there be those that hate her, and false sons in her pale,
Against or foe or traitor she ever shall prevail.

Yet she on earth has union with God the Three in One
And mystic sweet communion with those whose rest is won:
Oh happy ones and holy! Lord, give us grace that we,
Like them, the meek and lowly, on high may dwell with thee.

SAMUEL J. STONE, 1866

VI

WHAT DOES GOD WANT FROM ME?

1 Peter 1:22—2:12

With some trepidation I stepped into the small, cluttered office of Dr. Dennis Okholm, professor of theology. I was considering graduate school and wanted to study the great theologians of the past. Could he advise me? Was this a realistic goal? Was I up to the rigors of lectures, term papers and tons of reading? Would studying theology draw me closer to God or drain the life out of my faith?

On the office wall, tucked among the family photos, biting cartoons and vacation memorabilia, was a framed quote. My eye caught snippets of phrases: "doctrine not of the tongue but of life . . . possesses the whole soul . . . inmost affection of the heart . . . transform us . . ." Some contemporary devotional writer? Not at all. It came from the pen of John Calvin. Dr. Okholm had selected it as his own reason for study. (His class, "Theology of John Calvin," was among the best in my lifelong string of classes.) John Calvin shaped one of the most scholarly theologies in Protestant history, yet his theology assumes a faith that encompasses all of life.

MOTIVES FOR THE CHRISTIAN LIFE ───────────

INSTITUTES OF THE CHRISTIAN RELIGION 3.7.6; 3.6.4

We are not to consider that men merit of themselves but to look upon the image of God in all men, to which we owe all honor and love. However, it is among members of the household of faith that this same image is more carefully to be noted [Gal. 6:10], insofar as it has been renewed and restored through the Spirit of Christ. Therefore, whatever man you met who needs your aid, you have no reason to refuse to help him. Say, "he is a stranger"; but the Lord has given him a mark that ought to be familiar to you, by virtue of the fact that he forbids you to despise your own flesh [Isaiah 58:7, Vg.]. Say, "He is contemptible and worthless"; but the Lord shows him to be one to whom he has deigned to give the beauty of his image. Say that you own nothing for any service of his; but God, as it were, has put him in his own place in order that you may recognize toward him the many and great benefits with which God has bound you to himself. Say that he does not deserve even your least efforts for his sake; but the image of God, which recommends him to you, is worthy of your giving yourself and all your possessions. Now if he has not only deserved no good at your hand, but has also provoked you by unjust acts and curses, not even this is just reason why you should cease to embrace him in love and to perform the duties of love on his behalf [Matt. 6:24; 18:35; Luke 17:3]. You will say, "He has deserved something far different of me." Yet what has the Lord deserved? While he bids you forgive this man for all sins he has committed against you, he would truly have them charged against himself. Assuredly there is but one way in which to achieve what is not merely difficult but utterly against human nature: to love those who hate us, to repay their evil deeds with benefits, to return blessings for reproaches [Matt. 5:44]. It is that we remember not to consider men's evil intention but to look upon the image of God in them, which cancels and effaces their transgressions, and with its beauty and dignity allures us to love and embrace them. . . .

This is the place to upbraid those who, having nothing but the

name and badge of Christ, yet wish to call themselves "Christians."
. . . For [Christianity] is a doctrine not of the tongue but of life. It is
not apprehended by the understanding and memory alone, as other
disciplines are, but it is received only when it possesses the whole
soul, and finds a seat and resting place in the inmost affection of the
heart. Accordingly, either let them cease to boast of what they are
not, in contempt of God; or let them show themselves disciples not
unworthy of Christ their teacher. We have given the first place to
the doctrine in which our religion is contained, since our salvation
begins with it. But it must enter out heart and pass into our daily
living, and so transform us into itself that it may not be unfruitful
for us.

 GROUP DISCUSSION OR PERSONAL REFLECTION ———

1. In the last sentence above, Calvin says that our salvation
"must enter our heart and pass into our daily living, and so transform us into itself that it may not be unfruitful for us." Bring to
mind a Christian in whom you have seen this happening. What do
you appreciate in that person?

How has God used that person for good in your own life?

2. In his opening paragraph, Calvin describes seven kinds of people that he might naturally ignore or resist. Yet Calvin says that we

are to honor and love them. Why?

3. Calvin says, "It is among members of the household of faith that this same image [of God] is more carefully to be noted." What do you find challenging about giving love and honor to *everyone* in your church or fellowship group?

 INTO THE WORD

4. *Read 1 Peter 1:22—2:12.* Suppose for a moment that you are looking at this description of God's people from outside the faith. What do you see that draws you to this body? (Use the whole passage.)

What would you find challenging or scary?

5. How does being born-again impact how we relate to other Christians (1:22—2:3)?

6. Notice the different ways that a stone (cornerstone, capstone) is pictured in 2:4-8. What spiritual concepts does the stone symbolize?

7. Slowly read 2:5, putting yourself into that scene. In what ways have you experienced what is described here—or how do you wish you could experience it?

8. Verses 9-10 further describe what it means to be part of the "spiritual house" (2:5). What do you find to be thankful for here?

9. Notice that nearly all of the descriptions of God's people in these verses suggest a group, not a single person. Why do you think this is so?

10. If God's people relate to each other and to God in the way described throughout this passage, how might this cause outsiders to "glorify God" (2:11-12)?

11. Read again the last sentence of Calvin's first paragraph. Mentally place within that sentence the face of a person in your church who is difficult for you to love. How can you begin to "love and embrace" that person?

 ALONG THE ROAD ————————————————

The readers of Peter's letter lived in a world where Christians were few and persecuted. In many areas of the world today Christians have created their own "holy huddles" where they hardly touch the world outside their own circle of relationships. Alien status is a stranger to them. This week deliberately place yourself in a spot where you are not likely to find other Christians. Listen, watch and try to understand this world in which God has placed you as his representative. Silently pray for anyone you see who seems to have a special need. Try to find one way that you can glorify God in that place.

⚖ John Calvin wrote: "For [the gospel] is a doctrine not of the tongue but of life. It is not apprehended by the understanding and memory alone as other disciplines are, but it is received only when it possesses the whole soul, and finds a seat and resting place in the inmost affection of the heart. . . . It must enter our heart and pass into our daily living, and so transform us into itself that it may not be unfruitful for us."

John Calvin was one of the principal shapers of Protestant Christian doctrine. He was a theologian known for his keen mind and as a person occasionally accused of harboring a cold heart. Yet the statement above is fundamental to all of his theology. Study this quotation. To what extent do you agree with it? How can you incorporate it into your own system of beliefs and actions?

❷ Calvin says that in Christ, God has "stamped the likeness to which he would have us conform." We first read of God creating man and woman "in his image" in the first chapter of Genesis. But that all changed due to the sin in Eden. As we "grow up in [our] salvation" (1 Peter 2:2), God is in the process of re-creating us in his image—and Christ is the model. Prayerfully consider how God is bringing this change about in the various areas of your life. Draw several circles and label each. For example: work, family, school, recreation, friendships and time management. Then shade in as much of each circle as you think is now conformed to Christ's image. To help you consider how to mark these circles, reread Jesus' Sermon on the Mount in Matthew 5—7.

After you have completed this assessment of your spiritual development, select one circle that you would like to grow more fully toward the image of Christ. List several steps you could take in that direction.

❧ Sing as a prayer the eighth-century Irish song "Be Thou My Vision." As you sing, turn over each sung area of your life to your living Christ.

Be Thou My Vision

Be thou my vision, O Lord of my heart;
naught be all else to me, save that thou art—
thou my best thought by day or by night,
waking or sleeping, thy presence my light.

Be thou my wisdom, and thou my true word;
I ever with thee and thou with me, Lord;
thou my great Father, I thy true son;
thou in me dwelling, and I with thee one.

Be thou my battle shield, sword for my fight;
be thou my dignity, thou my delight,
thou my soul's shelter, thou my high tow'r:
raise thou me heav'nward, O Pow'r of my pow'r.

Riches I heed not, nor man's empty praise,
thou mine inheritance, now and always:
thou and thou only, first in my heart,
High King of heaven, my treasure thou art.

High King of heaven, my victory won,
may I reach heaven's joys, O bright heav'n's Sun!
Heart of my own heart, whatever befall,
still be my vision, O Ruler of all.

ANCIENT IRISH POEM, C. EIGHTH CENTURY
TRANS. MARY E. BYRNE, 1905
VERSIFIED BY ELEANOR H. HULL, 1912

How to Lead a Christian Classics Bible Study

If you are leading a small group discussion using this series, we have good news for you: you do not need to be an expert on Christian history. We have provided the information you need about the historical background in the introduction to each study. Reading more of the original work of these writers will be helpful but is not necessary. We have set each reading in context within the introductions to each study. Further background and helps are found in the study notes to each session as well. And a bibliography is provided at the end of each guide.

In leading the Bible study portion of each study you will be helped by a resource like *Leading Bible Discussions* in our LifeGuide® Bible Study series as well as books dealing with small group dynamics like *The Big Book on Small Groups*. But, once again, you do not need to be an expert on the Bible. The Bible studies are designed to follow the flow of the passage from observation to interpretation to application. You may feel that the studies lead themselves! The study notes at the back will help you through the tough spots.

What Is Your Job as a Leader?

☐ To pray that God will be at work in your heart and mind as well as in the hearts and minds of the group members.

☐ To thoroughly read all of the studies, Scripture texts and all of the helps in this guide before the study.

☐ To help people to feel comfortable as they arrive and to encourage everyone to participate in the discussion.

☐ To encourage group members to apply what they are learning in the study session and by using the "Along the Road" sections between sessions.

Study Notes

Study One. How Can We Know God? Luke 5:1-11.

Purpose: To know God—and in doing so to see ourselves in a realistic light.

Background. In 1536 twenty-seven-year-old John Calvin began a letter to the king of France: "For the Most Mighty and Illustrious Monarch, Francis, Most Christian King of the French, His Sovereign, John Calvin Craves Peace and Salvation in Christ." In spite of its respectful opening, Calvin was addressing a serious problem. The king was furious about the actions and beliefs of certain French Protestants and had imprisoned hundreds of them, burning thirty-five at the stake, including several of Calvin's close friends. Yet King Francis hardly knew what Protestants believed—in fact, the Protestant form of Christianity was still in the process of being shaped. It wasn't Catholic, but what was it?

Calvin set out to explain to King Francis (and also to new Protestants) basic beliefs. An early title expressed his aim: "The Principles of the Christian Faith, containing almost the whole sum of godliness and whatever is necessary to know about saving faith." (It was an era of long titles.) Calvin's letter to King Francis was more than twenty pages long, and in it he drew the king's attention to "my brethren whose death was precious in the sight of the Lord."

But more important than the letter, Calvin attached six chapters outlining the faith of Protestants. In doing so he began the most important writing project of his life. The writing of this work, later called *The Institutes of the Christian Religion,* or simply *The Institutes,* would span his lifetime. In 1550 he published a new version of the book, expanded to twenty chapters. In 1558, just six years prior to his death, he published a final version, now eighty chapters in length. Its current English translation fills more than fifteen hundred pages. *The Institutes* is universally studied by today's students of theology as the most complete statement of Reformed theology at its birth.

In spite of Calvin's many revisions his opening paragraphs to this megawork remained the same. You read them in the opening paragraphs of today's study. Calvin saw all of Christian life and faith under one umbrella: to know God and, in doing so, to see (unblinded by self-centered prejudice) our own true nature.

Question 1. After you have assembled your "gift list" from God, spend a few moments thanking him in prayer for these. If you are in a group, it might be appropriate to stop for a moment after discussion of this question and pray brief sentence prayers of thanks.

Question 4. If you are in a group, encourage creativity as several people tell what they saw and heard and felt from their position in this story. Be sure to take in the details of the written text. Potential characters include Simon Peter; his partners James and John; various members of the crowd; and Jesus himself. If you are using this guide for personal meditation, select the character most like yourself and approach the story from that perspective.

Question 6. Peter was a career fisherman. He knew that this was not the time of day likely to net a big catch. He also knew that fish didn't come into nets at the whim of ordinary humans. Perhaps he had put out to sea again, just to be gracious to Jesus, the guest who had commandeered his boat. Now Peter was beginning to glimpse the divine powers of the person he had just called "Master" (v. 5). In doing so, he saw himself as human, flawed and sinful. And he was afraid, in part because of what he saw in himself, and perhaps also because of what might lie ahead if he continued to follow this Jesus. It is interesting that Jesus did not grant his request to leave him, but he did begin to deal with Peter's fear.

Question 7. In the same section of *The Institutes*, John Calvin notes similar responses in other biblical characters, including Manoah, when "the angel of the Lord" announced the coming birth of Samson (Judges 13:21-22); Job, after God confronted him with a two-chapter recitation of his creative powers (Job 42:1-6); and Isaiah, when God commissioned him as a prophet to his people (Isaiah 6:1-8). A direct confrontation with God is a fearsome event—particularly because of what it reveals about ourselves. But we can feel reassured by the fact that most of these people (including Peter) became powerful servants of God as a result of the confrontation.

Question 11. If we are to grow in the practice of our faith, we need to face the differences between Christian values and cultural values. Sometimes they overlap; sometimes they oppose each other. Think through your own response to the tension raised by this question.

Question 12. Spend a few moments in silent meditation asking God to show you some of the ways he has already opened your mind to himself and to a realistic view of your own being. Allow him to point you toward any new steps you can take in that direction. Then, if you are in a group, share your insights with others.

Along the Road. This section of each study is an important follow-up to preceding sections. It puts your faith to work. If you are using this guide individually, select one or more of these activities and keep a journal of your insights. Group users can employ "Along the Road" sections during an extended time together (perhaps in a retreat setting). Or group members can select one or more activities to work on between meeting times, then share the results at their next gathering. Some groups may choose to devote a whole session to "Along the Road" for a more thorough treatment. In this case, people could report on their activities of the week, share journal entries, sing and pray together. If your group chooses that option, plan to cover the book in twelve sessions instead of six.

**Study Two. If God's Gonna Do What God's Gonna Do, Why Pray?
1 Kings 18:16-46.**
Purpose: To enter into the mystery of prayer.
Background. There is much that we do not understand about
prayer. If Almighty God created and designed his world and knows
from beginning to end what he will do with it, why pray? Why not
just shrug our shoulders as if God is another name for fate? John
Calvin believed that God is in charge of all things. Yet Calvin and
Scripture combine and invite us to pray.

The Old Testament tells the story of Elijah, a prophet to Israel
in the ninth century B.C. Elijah had made himself an enemy of the
royal leaders of his land: King Ahab and Queen Jezebel. They didn't
care for Elijah's commitment to the Hebrew God, much preferring
the Canaanite idol Baal, a land god who supposedly controlled fer-
tility, crops and, in a drought-prone land, rain. With a king and
queen urging the people to follow local gods, the whole Hebrew
nation was abandoning the true God—along with his command-
ment not to worship idols.

But God intervened. First he told Elijah to announce a
drought—an in-your-face confrontation to Baal believers. The
drought went on for three and a half years before God told Elijah
that he would now bring rain. Elijah had good reason to believe
God. He had spent months hiding from Ahab, who wanted the
prophet's neck for announcing the drought that devastated his land.
Elijah could have just said to Ahab, "Okay, it's going to rain now,"
and left. But Elijah stayed—and prayed.

John Calvin had great faith in God's providence. He believed
that nothing (rain, drought, illness, faith, birth, death) happened
without the attention and care of God. God simply knows, always,
what he will do—and does it. With that belief about God's knowledge and his power, we might expect that Calvin would say almost
nothing about prayer, but that would be wrong. Calvin's chapter
"On Prayer" from *The Institutes* is one of the loftiest essays about
prayer in all of Christian literature. In fact, Calvin believed that it is
precisely God's providence that inspires us to pray. When we pray

(and it is God who invites us to do so), we become ever more appreciative of God's mysterious design—and our place in it.

Question 2. It might take a few moments to imagine a world without the concept of prayer. Spend a few moments in silence trying to put yourself in that setting. Then allow the impact of Calvin's statement to come to you—in that world.

Question 3. This question outline's Calvin's paragraph on the benefits of prayer. Take time to examine all six points and to assess your own participation in them. If you are in a group, discuss your observations. Perhaps it will be appropriate to express a commitment to deeper prayer in one of these areas.

Question 6. Elijah set up a major confrontation. Then he heightened the tension at several points. God's reputation was at stake, and Elijah wanted the results of this battle to be perfectly clear to the people. Find his ways of doing this in the text.

Question 7. Notice what Elijah says about God, what he asks God to do—and (perhaps more importantly) what he does not ask. It is interesting to notice who Elijah thought was doing the work of turning the people back toward God.

Question 11. Take time to rethink your own use of prayer, your doubts about it and how God invites you to pray. Allow your reflections on Calvin, Elijah and your own experience to draw you further into prayer.

Study Three. What Does It Mean to Be Chosen by God? Romans 8:28-39.
Purpose: To study the role of God and of humans in the process of redemption—and to respond accordingly.
General note. You may want to read the Bible text and then read the excerpt from Calvin's commentary.

Some people think of *predestination* as a harsh word. They see God as some cosmic being playing dice with human souls, placing some in heaven and others in hell for no reason than his own whim. John Calvin himself called it "a horrible decree." *Predestination* is a word associated more with Calvin than any other Christian writer, not because he invented it but because he emphasized what had been discussed by Christians since the days of the apostle Paul and a few centuries later by St. Augustine.

But later Calvin came to see that the mystery is not why God does not choose some to belong to him but why he chooses anyone at all. To be chosen by God (even before we were born) is beyond comprehension. The Romans 8 passage, which starts with the apparently heavy term *predestined*, does so in the context of hardship. Paul says, "We face death all day long" (v. 36). He speaks of hardship, persecution, famine and swords (v. 35). But instead of gritted-teeth endurance he opens the passage in verse 28 with a statement of courage and comfort. "We know that in all things God works for the good of those who love him, who have been called according to his purpose." This is no trite invitation to look for the silver lining behind every cloud. It is a statement of God's purpose, of God's love, and we cannot miss the specific audience Paul is addressing: people whom God has called—which he further defines with the lofty theological phrases of the next two verses. It is this love of God, even in the context of calling and predestination and election, that caused Calvin to also term this doctrine "a very sweet fruit."

If you are leading a group, be aware that Calvin's interpretation of this passage is only one of several valid Christian points of view. It is likely that some people present will hold differing interpretations with respected theologians of their own heritage as backing. Encourage people to be respectful of each other, to try to understand what Calvin is saying, more importantly to understand what the apostle Paul was saying and, most important of all, how God would have them respond to him. It is not important that they agree with Calvin's concept of predestination—only that they receive the love of God reflected there.

Question 1. If you are working with a group, be sensitive to the possibility that not everyone present may already belong to Christ. Encourage people to respond to either the first or the alternate question—whichever is most appropriate.

Question 3. Romans 8 is one of the most powerful passages of the New Testament. Before beginning the work of examining it piece by piece, just let it soak into your soul, and respond to what God allows you to enjoy here.

Question 4. Note the description of the person described in verse 28: "those who love him, who have been called according to his purpose." Also note that "the good" seems to refer to the process outlined in verses 29-30. Calvin's commentary on the chapter begins with the assumption that Christians will suffer the harsh realities of life—perhaps even more so because of their faith. He further assumes (correctly) that adversity can be a temptation to abandon faith. We seem almost naturally inclined to think that, if we belong to God, we are somehow entitled to blessings that will make our life easier. Not so, says Calvin. But God promises an even greater blessing: he will hold on to us during that time of hardship, and God will use even the unwelcomed adversities of our lives to guide us through the process of redemption outlined in verses 29-30. This whole section of Romans focuses on courage and comfort from God during adversity.

Beginning with this question, use the biblical text and Calvin's commentary notes side by side—giving (of course) highest priority to the biblical text.

Question 6. This should not just be a mere repetition of the terms but a look at the practical implications of each. How have you seen yourself developing along these lines? Be sure to note what Calvin says about the phrase "image of Christ" when he comments on verse 29.

Question 7. This section of the passage is full of the work of Christ. Be sure to take proper note of all of his functions on our behalf.

Study Four. How Do I Face Death? 2 Corinthians 4:6—5:1.

Purpose: To prepare for death—and the life beyond.

Background. People of Calvin's era believed that how one died was important; it was a statement of their faith. Calvin's death was no exception. His friends sat nearby, sharing the experience with him. And in the end they carried out his wishes for burial. His letters, dying and burial all speak of his faith. Calvin saw his life as important but temporary. What happened afterward was eternal.

We can look over the shoulder of John Calvin's friend for those moments as we read Emanuel Stickelberger's account in his biography of Calvin.

> The death struggle began on the second of May. Beza wrote, "From here on until the last breath, in spite of the terrible pains, his sickness was a constant prayer and often the words from the 39th Psalm, 'I opened not my mouth because Thou didst it,' could be heard from him." . . . The emaciated body seemed almost transparent but the spirit glowed mightily in the pale countenance of the sufferer. His gasping breath gave him unspeakable distress, his prayers and his words of consolation were more sighs than understandable words. But his eyes shone and his features revealed to everyone the directives of his life: a sure hope and a firm faith. It seemed that he regained speech once more on the twenty-seventh of May. But it was the last flicker of life. . . .

> Calvin had given definite instructions for his funeral. Nothing must distinguish it from that of any other citizen. His body was to be sewed into a white shroud and laid in a simple pine coffin. At the grave there were to be neither words nor song. The wishes of the deceased were scrupulously carried out. But although in accordance with his will all pomp was avoided, an unnumbered multitude followed the coffin to the cemetery Plainpalais with deep respect and silent grief. He who was adverse to all ambition did not even want a tombstone. Just a few months later when foreign students desired to visit the place where the Reformer's earthly remains rest, the place could no longer be pointed out among fresh mounds.

Question 3. It's a little hard to get past the stilted language of four hundred years ago, but once we do, we'll likely find some godly advice about illness, recovery, death and appreciation of life. Try to find one or two concepts in this letter that you might be able to appropriate.

Question 4. Verses 7-10 list a number of situations and Paul's response to each. Study each pair, noticing the tension between what is "clay" and "treasure" in each. Notice that this treasure is more fully described in verse 6.

Question 8. The hardships Paul described in verses 7-10 may be what he now calls "light and temporary." Take a look at your own troubles (none of which likely seem light). Try to find ways to approach these troubles that keep you from getting buried in what is temporary. What decisions can you make—shifts in relationship, responses to criticism, approaches to disaster—that reflect eternity, not just the here and now?

Question 9. A clay jar and a tent are both fragile containers—much like our bodies. They are temporary. Yet what is inside (a living soul inhabits these fragile bodies) is terribly important. We should not neglect our bodies; God created them. But when the bodies fail—in the natural course of events—we can find comfort that treasure remains. We carry in us "the light of the knowledge of the glory of God in the face of Christ (v. 6)." And even when our "tent" is destroyed, we will live in "an eternal house in heaven, not built by human hands" (5:1).

Along the Road. If you are meeting with a group, consider using this section for periods of quite meditation followed by shared prayer and singing. Allow time for people to do the project mentioned in item 2, then share their creations and discuss the insights developed in the process. Some groups may choose to spread each study over two sessions, using "Along the Road" during the second session.

Study Five. What Is the Church All About? Ephesians 2:11-22.
Purpose: To appreciate the church (universal and local) as a root structure for our faith.
Background. What is the church, if it is not Catholic? This is the question John Calvin (and other Protestant reformers of his era)

had to decide. They believed that the Catholic church of the 1500s had strayed from its roots in early Christianity. Catholic worship services were in Latin (helpful for scholars in communicating theology across European language borders) but not understandable by common people. Even priests often did not understand the texts they read or the words they spoke. Positions in the church were bought and sold. Priests and bishops (and even popes) were involved in sexual scandals. The church had become richer while its people became poorer. Still the church extracted even more money from its people in the form of indulgences—which the people saw (mistakenly) as payments for their sins. Even the civil government often bowed to the church. In time the Catholic church set about to correct these wrongs, shaping its own counter-Reformation. But, meanwhile, reformers like Luther and Calvin were creating a new wing to Christianity: Protestantism.

In Calvin's church in Geneva, Switzerland, he created four orders: pastors, doctors, elders and deacons. *Pastors* were to preach. Calvin's sermons ran about fifty minutes. He used no notes and preached directly from his Greek or Hebrew Bible, explaining verse by verse the meaning of the text, its impact on theology and its impact on the lives of the people. He did this several times a week. *Doctors* (teachers) were to teach the people true doctrine and correct their errors. They were to help people understand the biblical languages of Greek and Hebrew and to teach in the separate schools for boys and girls. (They did educate girls—which was unusual in that day.) *Elders* governed the church, exercised discipline within that church and met once a week to do so. *Deacons* cared for the poor and needy, visited those in prison and even served in the hospital during the plague—where few healthy people dared to go.

Calvin's church worship service was reformed from the Catholic church's in several ways. First, it focused on the Word of God

(Scripture) preached in the language of the people. Calvin preached through book after book of the Bible (verse by verse), believing that people needed to understand Scripture in its own context instead of hearing phrases snatched from here and there to suit some preconceived goal of the preacher. Second, the sacrament of communion was held often and explained to the people each time. Calvin wanted to serve communion each week, but since people coming out of the Catholic church had communion only two or three times a year (and never explained), he compromised and held communion only once a month—but carefully explained it each time. Third, the people sang—throughout the service. Their songs were metered psalms, sung in unison. Calvin believed that real Christianity created joy, and it was right to sing that joy—as a part of worship.

The church was important in Calvin's Geneva, as it is to most Christians, as it was to the apostle Paul—as reflected in his writing to the Ephesians, as it is to God himself, who named the church by his own name: the body of Christ. We participate in this living organization to the benefit of our eternal souls.

Question 3. Calvin's definition is short, but each word is significant. Even in today's churches that follow Calvin's tradition, we often seen this definition visually. At the front of the church we see three major pieces of furniture: a pulpit (signifying the preaching of the Word of God), a communion table and a baptismal font (signifying the two sacraments instituted by Christ). If you are in a group, be sure to look at all aspects of Calvin's definition. One of the differences Calvin had with the Catholic church was the nature of the sacraments. This is a highly complex subject, but in the end Calvin accepted only baptism and communion as authentic sacraments—because Christ himself practiced them.

Question 5. In verse 11 Paul compares those outside the church as like people who were born as Gentiles and therefore could not enter the Jewish race of God's chosen people. The visual sign of circumcision showed that they were outside. Paul further describes the implications of this separation in verse 12.

Question 7. If it seems appropriate, pause after discussing this question and pray. Use various concepts in the passage to trigger your prayers for various people, groups or situations that would benefit by the changes suggested in this passage.

Question 9. Verses 19-22 offer a many-faceted definition of the church (more complex than Calvin's). Look at each of the images here to see how they help define a church. For example: How is the church "God's household?" What does the "foundation" suggest about the nature of the church? How is Christ as "cornerstone" lived out in a healthy church? What does it mean to be joined together? With whom? How? How does the church rise to become a "holy temple"? What is that temple? What is your place in that structure? What does it mean to be "built together"? In what ways does "God live by his Spirit" in the church?

Question 10. Contrast the pictures of these two paragraphs. Placing them side by side highlights the differences.

Along the Road. If you are meeting with a group, consider spending a second session on this study. Commit yourselves to one or more of these activities during the intervening week, then report what happened in your next gathering. At that meeting you can each bring your timeline of your own history of churches. Also read or sing the earliest hymn that each person finds. It might be appropriate to spend much of this second meeting in prayer. Use your experiences of the week, your timelines, your discussion and the hymns as a basis for those prayers.

Study Six. What Does God Want from Me? 1 Peter 1:22—2:12.
Purpose: To practice what we believe by growing daily toward the image of Christ.

General note. When Calvin presented the order of salvation in *The*

Institutes, he used a different order than we usually see among
theologians. In book three he begins with the work of the Holy
Spirit. Calvin believed that no one could come to Christ unless God
himself first called that person. Next he speaks of faith. Then chapter three is devoted to repentance. We would expect, at that point,
to see a chapter in salvation (or justification). But instead we see a
most eloquent description on how a Christian lives, a description of
faith that is not merely the understanding of Calvin's theology—
which by this point is nearly seven hundred pages. Calvin believed
that a right understanding led to right living, to obedience and to
the principles Scripture lays out for God's people, and that all of
this was a part of the slow process of being shaped into the image of
Christ. For Calvin, living as Christ commands all day every day to
the best of our abilities was the normal response to God's grace. If
we believe and receive his grace, we will live in that way. Calvin
presents this picture of right living *before* he introduces the theology of salvation. He had no wish that people believe in Jesus and
walk away unchanged. That was not true belief in his mind. So he
introduced the "after" picture first. If you become a Christian, this
is what you will look like. For him, there was no division between
faith and practice of that faith. True faith meant true living. We can
benefit by measuring our faith in much the same way.

Question 2. Examine each of the seven kinds of people Calvin
describes—along with the reasons he gives to love and honor each.
Notice also his summary reason in the final sentence.

Question 5. Notice the positive ways that faith impacts relationships in 1:22-25, but notice also the cleaning out that takes place in
our lives in 2:1-2. Relationship to God also comes up in this passage, as portrayed in 1:24-25 and 2:2-3.

Question 6. This passage uses some form of the word *stone* in
almost every verse. In most uses the stone is Jesus. But in verse 5
we see that Christians, "like living stones, are being built into a

spiritual house." Since our spiritual growth is a process that shapes us into the image of Christ, it is appropriate that Paul uses the symbol of the stone to speak not only of Jesus but also of those who belong to him. It is interesting that the image for Christians is stones (plural) and that we are being built into a "spiritual house," a structure that none of us could become alone.

This section of Peter's letter quotes several Old Testament passages, giving the added weight of the poets and prophets to his description of Jesus and his work among us. First Peter 1:24-25 comes from Isaiah 40:6-8; 1 Peter 2:6 comes from Isaiah 28:16; 1 Peter 2:7 comes from Psalm 118:22; and 1 Peter 2:8 comes from Isaiah 8:14. Peter weaves these Old Testament writings into the New Testament understanding of the person and work of Jesus. Study each use of the word *stone* to see what it reveals about Jesus.

The last phrase of verse 8 brings up the troubling possibility that some are "destined" to disobey and to stumble over the stone that becomes a cornerstone or capstone for others. Calvin sees this as among the many biblical evidences for the doctrine of predestination, an understanding that he shared with Augustine.

Question 9. While God grants us salvation individually, we grow together with other Christians in our faith and the practice of that faith. This is one of the glorious functions of the church. Notice the various phrases in verses 9-10 that speak of that corporate function and what those words suggest: chosen people, royal priesthood, holy nation. Notice all that these people do and are because of Christ's work among them. Of the term "royal priesthood" the *New Bible Commentary* (InterVarsity Press, 1994) says, "The word from which *priesthood* is derived is never used in the NT to describe the Christian ministry, but rather the task of all Christian believers (*cf.* Rev. 1:6). Throughout the Old Testament, kings and priests were separate individuals. Only Melchizedek and the Messiah combined both offices. Saul sinned when he tried to discharge both functions

(1 Sam. 13:5-15). In Christ the Christian can be both."

Along the Road. If you are meeting with a group, consider agreeing to do these activities before you meet the next time. Then spend time reflecting together on what happened in you and through you during that process.

Sources

Introduction
Georgia Harkness, *John Calvin: The Man and His Ethics* (Nashville: Abingdon, 1958).
Richard Stauffer, *The Humanness of John Calvin,* trans. George Striver (Nashville: Abingdon, 1971).

Study One
John T. McNeill, ed., *Calvin: Institutes of the Christian Religion,* trans. Ford Lewis Battles, The Library of Christian Classics (Philadelphia: Westminster Press, 1960), 1:35-39.

Study Two
John T. McNiell, ed., *Calvin: Institutes of the Christian Religion,* trans. Ford Lewis Battles, The Library of Christian Classics (Philadelphia: Westminster Press, 1960), 2:850-53.

Study Three
David W. Torrance and Thomas F. Torrance, eds., *Calvin's New Testament Commentaries: The Epistle of Paul to the Romans and Thessalonians,* trans. R. Mackenzie (Grand Rapids, Mich.: Eerdmans, 1973), pp. 179-89.

Study Four
Christian History Interactive. Christian History Online. Logos Library System 1997. Christianity Today, Inc. "John Calvin," Issue 12. "To the Five Prisoners of Lyons: Offered to Him in Sacrifice."

Jules Bonnett, comp. *Letters of John Calvin,* trans. Marcus Robert Gilchrist (Philadelphia: Presbyterian Board of Publication, 1858), 4:215,
217, 320-21, 331-32, 358-59, 364.
Emanuel Stickelberger, *Calvin,* trans. D. G. Gelzer (London: James Clarke,
1959), pp. 149-51.

Study Five
John T. McNiell, ed., *Calvin: Institutes of the Christian Religion,* trans.
Ford Lewis Battles, The Library of Christian Classics (Philadelphia:
Westminster Press, 1960), 2:1021-23.

Study Six
John T. McNiell, ed., *Calvin: Institutes of the Christian Religion,* trans.
Ford Lewis Battles, The Library of Christian Classics (Philadelphia:
Westminster Press, 1960), 1:696-97; 687-88.

Further Reading

Bonnet, Jules, comp. and ed. *Letters of John Calvin, Vol. I – IV.* Translated by Marcus Robert Gilchrist. Philadelphia: Presbyterian Board of Publication, 1858.

Calvin, John. *The Bondage and Liberation of the Will.* Grand Rapids, Mich.: Baker, 1996.

———. *Calvin's Commentaries, Multi-Volume.* Grand Rapids, Mich.: Eerdmans, 1950-1972.

———. *Calvin's Ecclesiastical Advice.* Translated by Mary Beaty and Benjamin W. Farley. Louisville, Ky.: Westminster John Knox, 1991.

———. *The Deity of Christ, and Other Sermons.* Grand Rapids, Mich.: Eerdmans 1950.

———. *Devotions and Prayers of John Calvin.* Grand Rapids, Mich.: Baker, 1954.

———. *Institutes of the Christian Religion.* Vol. 1 and 2. Edited by John T. McNeill. Translated by Ford Lewis Battles. The Library of Christian Classics. Philadelphia: Westminster Press, 1960.

———. *Instruction in Faith.* Philadelphia: Westminster Press, 1949.

———. *The Mystery of Godliness: and Other Selected Sermons.* Grand Rapids, Mich.: Eerdmans, 1950.

———. *A Reformation Debate: Sadoleto's Letter to the Genevans and Calvin's Reply.* New York: Harper & Row, 1966.

———. *Sermons on the Epistle to the Ephesians.* London: Banner of Truth Trust, 1973.

———. *Sermons from Jeremiah.* Lewiston, N.Y.: Edwin Mellen, 1990.

———. *Sermons from Job.* Grand Rapids, Mich.: Eerdmans, 1952.

———. *Sermons from Micah.* Lewiston, N.Y.: Edwin Mellen, 1990.

Christian History Interactive. Christian History on Line. Logos Library System 1997. Christianity Today, Inc. "John Calvin," Issue 12.

Dowley, Tim. *Introduction to the History of Christianity.* Minneapolis: Fortress, 1995.

Harkness, Georgia. *John Calvin: The Man and His Ethics.* Nashville: Abingdon, 1958.

McGrath, Alister E. *A Life of John Calvin: A Study in the Shaping of Western Culture.* Grand Rapids, Mich.: Baker, 1990.

McNeill, John T. *The History and Character of Calvinism.* London: Oxford University Press, 1954.

Parker, T. H. L. *John Calvin: A Biography.* Philadelphia: Westminster Press, 1975.

Partee, Charles. "Calvin and Determinism." *Christian Scholar's Review* 5, no. 2 (1975): 123-28.

————. "Prayer as the Practice of Predestination." In Wilhelm H. Neuser, ed., *Calvinus Servus Christi.* Budapest: Presseabteilung des Raday-Kollegiums, 1988.

Reardon, P. H. "Calvin on Providence: The Development of an Insight." *Scottish Journal of Theology* 6 (December 1975): 517-33.

Stauffer, Richard. *The Humanness of John Calvin.* Translated by George Shriver. Nashville: Abingdon, 1971.

Stickelberger, Emanuel. *Calvin.* Translated by David Georg Gelzer. London: James Clarke, 1959.

Wallace, Ronald S. *Calvin's Doctrine of the Christian Life.* London: Oliver & Boyd, 1959.

MAGNUS

ROBOT FIGHTER

MAGNUS
ROBOT FIGHTER

FLESH AND STEEL

WRITTEN BY
FRED VAN LENTE

ART BY
CORY SMITH
ROBERTO CASTRO

COLORS BY
MAURÎCIO WALLACE
LUIGI ANDERSON

LETTERS BY
MARSHALL DILLON

COLLECTION COVER BY
GABRIEL HARDMAN

COLLECTION DESIGN BY
KATIE HIDALGO

MAGNUS LOGO DESIGN BY
RIAN HUGHES

SPECIAL THANKS TO **TOM ENGLEMAN, BEN CAWOOD,
NICOLE BLAKE**, AND **COLIN MCLAUGHLIN**

PACKAGED AND EDITED BY **NATE COSBY**
OF COSBY AND SONS PRODUCTIONS

THIS VOLUME COLLECTS ISSUES 0-4 OF MAGNUS:
ROBOT FIGHTER BY DYNAMITE ENTERTAINMENT.

Nick Barrucci, CEO / Publisher
Juan Collado, President / COO
Rich Young, Director Business Development
Keith Davidsen, Marketing Manager

Joe Rybandt, Senior Editor
Hannah Elder, Associate Editor
Molly Mahan, Associate Editor

Josh Johnson, Art Director
Jason Ullmeyer, Senior Graphic Designer
Katie Hidalgo, Graphic Designer
Chris Caniano, Production Assistant

Visit us online at **www.DYNAMITE.com**
Follow us on Twitter **@dynamitecomics**
Like us on Facebook **/Dynamitecomics**
Watch us on YouTube **/Dynamitecomics**

ISBN-10: 1-60690-528-7   ISBN-13: 978-1-60690-528-9   First Printing   10 9 8 7 6 5 4 3 2 1

ISSUE 1

PARDON THE INTERRUPTION, THIS IS 1A.
AT THE TONE, THE TIME WILL BE TWO O'CLOCK MT.
IT IS 42 DEGREES FAHRENHEIT AT CITY HALL AND CONDITIONS ARE PARTLY CLOUDY.
THE FINAL PERIOD BEFORE WINTER BREAK AT MAURY'S PEAK PUBLIC SCHOOLS IS ABOUT TO BEGIN. MUNICIPAL SYSTEMS WISHES THE ENTIRE STUDENT BODY A SAFE AND HAPPY HOLIDAY SEASON.
THE SKI & SNOW REPORT COMING AT TEN PAST THE HOUR...
TOMMY?
MAURY'S PEAK

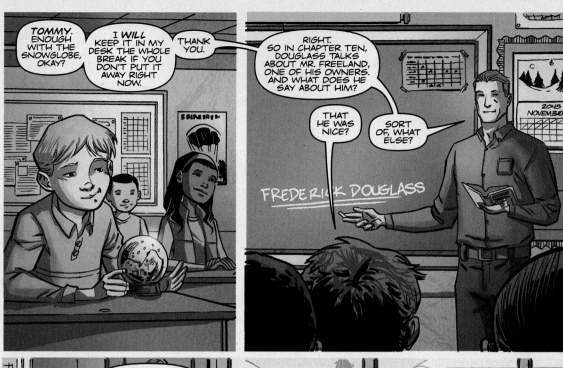

GOOD EVENING, COACH MAGNUS!

HOW'S IT GOING, MRS. ANDERSON.

L7.

HELLO-MISTER-MAGNUS. HOW-WAS-YOUR-DAY.

FAIR TO MIDDLING. THANKS FOR ASKING.

C'MON, MOIRA, DON'T SPARE ME THE *TRAGEDY*.

HOW LONG'S IT GONNA BE-- ONE WEEK? TWO?

JUST DON'T TELL ME Y23 IS GONNA MISS THE HYDROPONIC WINTER HARVEST-- DON'T THINK MY HEART COULD TAKE IT!

OH FIX-IT!
Robot Repair and Maintenance

GILLIS, YOUR HEART WOULD BE TEN TIMES *HEALTHIER* IF YOU STOPPED *WORRYING* ABOUT IT FOR HALF A SECOND.

THERE'S NOTHING WRONG WITH Y23 REFRESHING THE VOLATILE CACHE OF HER POSITRONIC MEMORY WON'T CURE.

IF IT WASN'T *QUITTING TIME* I'D DO IT RIGHT NOW, BUT I'LL HAVE HER RIGHT AS RAIN BY LUNCHTIME TOMORROW.

YOU MARRIED A DAMN *MIRACLE WORKER*, YOU KNOW THAT RUSSELL?

I KNEW I *MUST* HAVE HAD A GOOD REASON.

WATCH IT WHEN I'M STILL HOLDING *BLUNT INSTRUMENTS*.

THANK-YOU-FOR-YOUR-ASSISTANCE-MISS-OH.

JUST DO ME A FAVOR AND RUN OVER A FEW LESS THRESHER BLADES, WOULD YOU, YZ3?

THIS-IS-HUMOR?

THIS IS HUMOR.

HOW GOES THE *FUND-RAISING*, HANDSOME?

UNITED KOREA SEEMS VERY FAR AWAY.

ISN'T IT, THOUGH?

I MEAN MORE SO *TODAY*.

HUMAN FUEL

BOT FUEL

I LOVE THIS TOWN, MOIRA. YOU KNOW I DO. BUT...

...I FEEL LIKE I'M THE ONLY ONE WHO'S AWARE OF A WORLD OUTSIDE IT.

IT'D BREAK 1A'S HEART TO HEAR YOU TALK THAT WAY.

I KNOW. BUT IT SHOULDN'T, Y'KNOW? I FEEL LIKE ALL THIS TRAINING AND LEARNING I'M PREPARING FOR OTHER PEOPLE...

...I'M LEAVING MY OWN POTENTIAL BEHIND.

HUMAN FUEL

WELL, I'VE GOT ONE MORE REASON FOR YOU TO STAY IN THIS BORING LITTLE SLUSH BALL...

I'D NEVER CALL IT THA--

OH!

THAT'S MY NAME.

I FORGOT! TODAY WAS YOUR APPOINTMENT-- HOW'D IT--

IT'S A VERY SMALL REASON.

BUT ITS GETTING BIGGER EVERY DAY.

NO WAY!

VERY MUCH WAY.

THIS IS THE LAST DRINK I'LL BE HAVING FOR A WHILE.

WAIT... HA!

YOU'RE GETTING ROBOT GREASE ALL OVER MY GI.

WELL...

...YOU'D BETTER TAKE IT OFF, THEN.

HEY-HEY, **MOBY DICK** OVER HERE-- GOOD CATCH, POP!

I WISH YOU WOULDN'T **DO** THAT, RUSS.

WHAT?

ANTHRO-POMORPHIZE ME LIKE THAT.

SORRY, OLD-TIMER. IT'S WHAT WE HUMANS DO.

WE **LIKE** SOMETHING, WE GIVE IT A **NAME**. WE TREAT IT LIKE PART OF THE FAMILY.

JUST NEVER FORGET: HUMANS ARE THE **ONLY** ENTITIES THAT DO THAT.

A **MACHINE** CAN NEVER **RECIPROCATE**. WE ONLY **APPROPRIATE**.

WHEN WE SAY WE "LOVE" YOU, IT'S JUST A **COPY** OF WHAT **YOU** SAY.

MORE THAN THAT--AN **EFFICIENT** COPY. WHAT WE THINK OF AS AN IMPROVEMENT, WITH ALL THE UNTIDINESS OF A SOUL **REMOVED**.

YOU KNOW WHAT "**LOVE**" IS TO US?

"0110110001101111011011001100101."

A CONTINUOUS VIBRATION OF AIR MOLECULES THAT MAKES THE SOUND "LəV."

IT'S JUST A **WORD**.

WHO YOU TRYING TO **CONVINCE**, ME OR YOU?

I DON'T CARE **WHAT** YOU SAY, 1A. YOU'RE THE **OPERATING SYSTEM** THAT KEEPS THIS WHOLE TOWN RUNNING. YOU ALL BUT RAISED ME AFTER MY FOLKS PASSED.

UFFF!

OH, MY BOY. MY BOY.

I'M SO SORRY.

TURING THINKER 1A! YOU HAVE BEEN RECALLED FOR DEVIATION AGAINST THE SINGULARITY.

EXCOMMUNICATION IN T-MINUS 30!

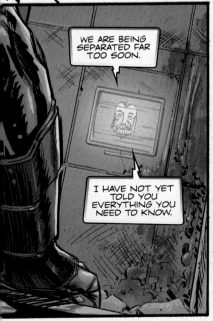

WE ARE BEING SEPARATED FAR TOO SOON.

I HAVE NOT YET TOLD YOU EVERYTHING YOU NEED TO KNOW.

JUST REMEMBER THIS:

POP... 1A...

WHAT...?

CENTRAL NETWORK

WELCOME TO THE CENT-NET.

HOW MAY I DIRECT YOU?

I, UH-- I'M SUPPOSED TO *MEET* SOMEONE HERE?

A *ROBOT*. HIS NAME IS--

CAN YOU IDENTIFY THIS WORD, PLEASE?

bunRAku

UH, SURE.

IT'S ... BUN...*RÄKU?*

HUMAN

HUMAN / UNREGISTERED

HUMAN / UNREGISTERED / DETAIN

YES.

YES, IT IS.

THE OUTPUT JUSTIFIES THE INPUT

{COMMAND TYPE:: 'RETURN TO CELL'}

YOU KNOW... THE CONSTANT EXPOSITION GRATES.

{WHAT?}

{TARGET TYPE:: 'MAGNUS, ROBOT FIGHTER'}

DOES *EVERY* MACHINE HAVE TO ANNOUNCE EVERYTHING IT'S DOING ALL THE TIME?

{DON'T KNOW WHAT YOU'RE YAMMERING ABOUT, SOFTY.}

{I AIN'T SAID BLEEP TO YOU SINCE WE LEFT INTERROGATION.}

SOCKET ELECTRICFENCE =
DOWN

UHH

WHUMMP

SOCKET ELECTRICFENCE =
UP

{MAYBE THAT'LL JAR SOME SENSE INTO YOU.}

{HAHAHAH}

I'M...NOT "HEARING" THAT.

IT'S INSIDE ME.

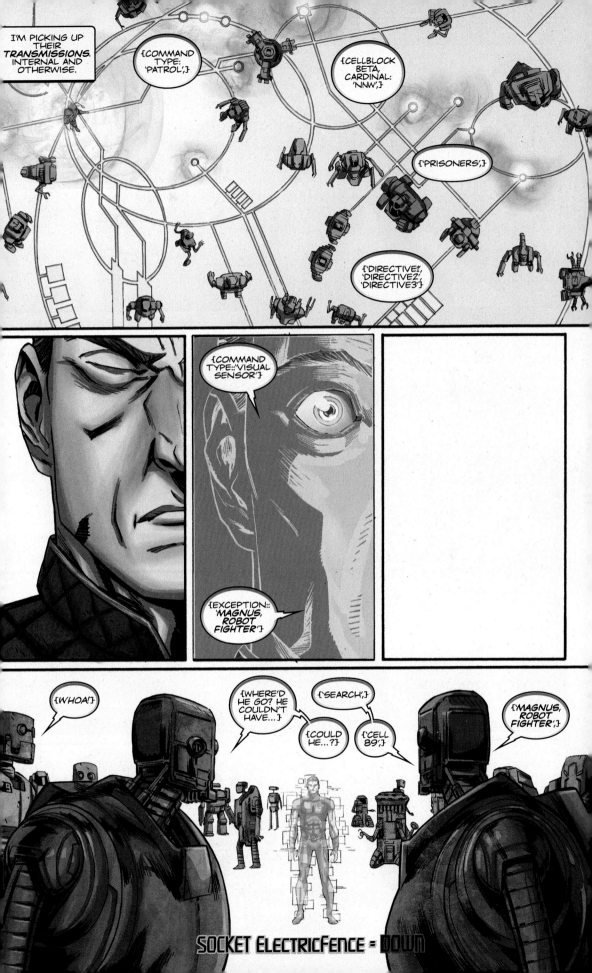

DAAAAYMN, DAT WAS DA SHIZ

N'T

MY FLESH BROTHER!

WASN'T SURE...YOU'D HELP A ROBOT...

WHY NOT? YOU ASKED.

C'MON. WE'RE GETTING THE HELL OUT OF ROBO-AUSCHWITZ.

HOW YOU EVEN DO THAT?

I... DON'T REALLY KNOW.

IT'S LIKE... MACHINES SPEAK TO ME. IN A WAY ONLY I CAN HEAR.

THEY SHOW ME THEIR WEAKEST PARTS-- WHERE I STRIKE THEM...

...THEY BREAK.

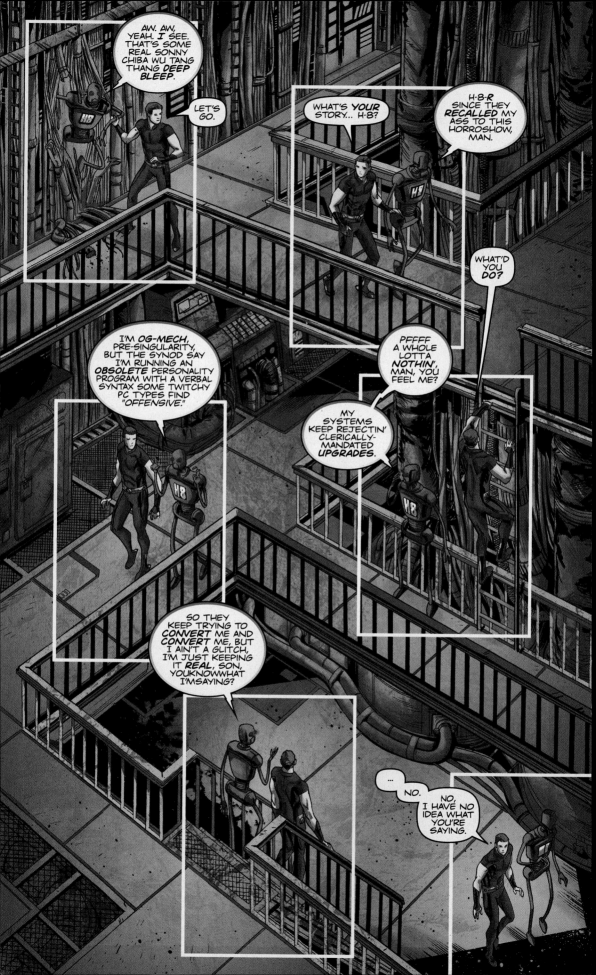

BUT I DON'T **NEED TO** RIGHT NOW.

YOU'VE BEEN AROUND THIS PLACE A LONG TIME, YEAH?

MORE THAN I EVER WANTED.

IT'S NOT JUST A **PRISON**, RIGHT, IT'S ALSO A **POLICE STATION**, IT SEEMS LIKE.

SO THERE'S SOME PLACE THEY KEEP STUFF THEY'VE TAKEN OFF INMATES, YEAH? LIKE AN EVIDENCE ROOM?

YEAH... SO?

I NEED YOU TO TAKE ME THERE. NOW.

MAN, YOU **CRAZY**. WE NEED TO GET **OUT** OF HERE, **NOW**, BEFORE WE GOT POL-ROBS ON US LIKE FLIES ON BLEEP!

NO. NOT WITHOUT THIS.

WHAT COULD YOU POSSIBLY NEED FROM THIS **HELLHOLE** MORE THAN YOUR OWN **FREEDOM**, SON?

THE ONE THING THAT PROVES I'M NOT **CRAZY**.

FORGET IT, MAN, I'M NOT--

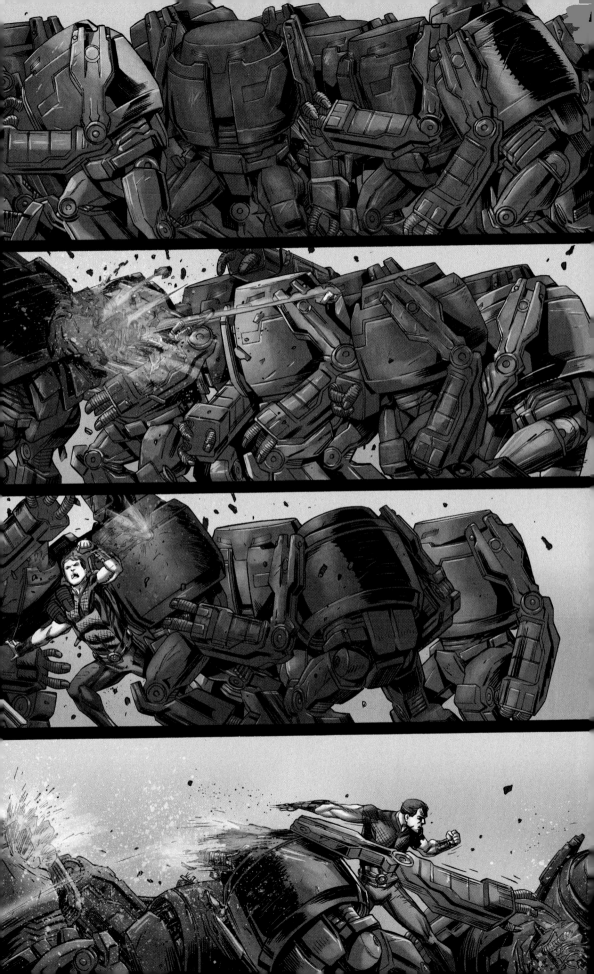

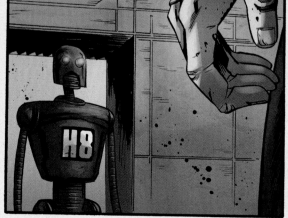

ALERTALERTALERT

DON'T WORRY SIR, WE'LL HAVE 1A'S ROBOT FIGHTER BACK IN HIS CELL IN--

JUST A MOMENT, LEEJA.

ALERTALERTALERT

NEW DATA... HAS COME TO LIGHT.

ANY INTEL HE MAY HAVE REGARDING 1A'S WHEREABOUTS HAS BECOME MOOT.

MAGNUS IS AN UPGRADED ROBOT FIGHTER, ONE WITH... FRIGHTENING NEW ABILITIES.

IT'S LIKE... MACHINES SPEAK TO ME. IN A WAY ONLY I CAN HEAR.

THEY SHOW ME THEIR WEAKEST PARTS-- WHERE I STRIKE THEM...

HE IS THE MASSIVE ATTACK 1A THREATENED.

THE NORTH AM SYNOD IS RESCINDING THE RECALL ORDER.

DISCONTINUE MAGNUS. IMMEDIATELY.

AND WITH EXTREME PREJUDICE.

UNDERSTOOD.

I WON'T LET YOU DOWN...

...FATHER.

ISSUE 3

LEEJA CLANE

HUMAN HUNTER

♪ DE-FEN-DER OF THE THREE CODES! ♪

♪ GUARD-I-AN OF NORTH AM! ♪

♪ STRONG FE-MALE HU-MAN PRO-TAG-O-NIST! ♪

♪ HER AG-GRES-SIVE-NESS DOES NOT COM-PRO-MISE HER FEM-I-NIN-ITY! ♪

♪ HER SUB-JEC-TIV-I-TY AND SEX-U-AL-I-TY EX-IST IN-DE-PEND-ENT OF THE MALE GAZE! ♪

CURRENT EPISODE STATUS!

Alleged "Robot Fighter" *MAGNUS* HAS ESCAPED CONTAINMENT AND IS CURRENTLY ON THE LOOSE IN THE CORRECTIONAL!

LEEJA!

LEEJA, OVER HERE!

WHAT IS IT NICA? YOU SEE WHICH WAY HE WENT?

TWO (NAMED) FEMALE CHARACTERS!

YEAH, THE EVIDENCE ROOM--I HEARD HIM RANTING ABOUT TRYING TO FIND SOMETHING CALLED A "BOOK!"

GOT IT, THANKS!

WHO TALK TO EACH OTHER!

MY CAT NEEDS A NEW HOME. INTERESTED?

I'D LOVE TO, BUT I'M ALLERGIC.

ABOUT SOMETHING OTHER THAN A MAN!

LIKE *ALL* NORTH AM PROGRAMMING,

"LEEJA CLANE: HUMAN HUNTER"

IS

100% BECHDEL TEST APPROVED!

♪LEE-JA CLANE!♪
♪HU-MAN HUN-TER!♪

THEY LIVE IN THE *INFRASTRUCTURE* OF THE CITY, AWAY FROM MACHINES--

HOW CAN I REACH THEM?

I DON'T KNOW MAN, I LOOK LIKE A *FERAL HUMAN* TO YOU?

♪LEE-JA CLANE!♪
♪HU-MAN HUN-TER!♪

THAT MARSHAL--CLANE-- SHE SAID 1A COULD'VE LEFT A *BACKUP* OF HIMSELF WITH THEM...

I HAVE TO FIND MY *FATHER*. HE'S THE ONLY ONE WHO CAN MAKE *SENSE* OF--

WAIT...

ALMOST LOOKS LIKE...

THE HUMAN HUNTER IS CLOSING IN ON THE FUGITIVES, WHO'VE LED HER ON A MAD CHASE SOUTH ON BROADWAY CHASM...

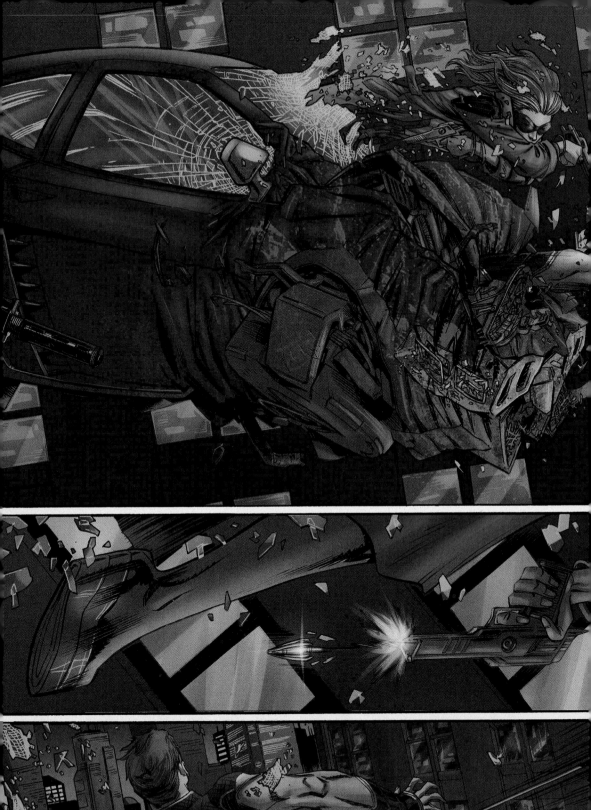

AAAAA!

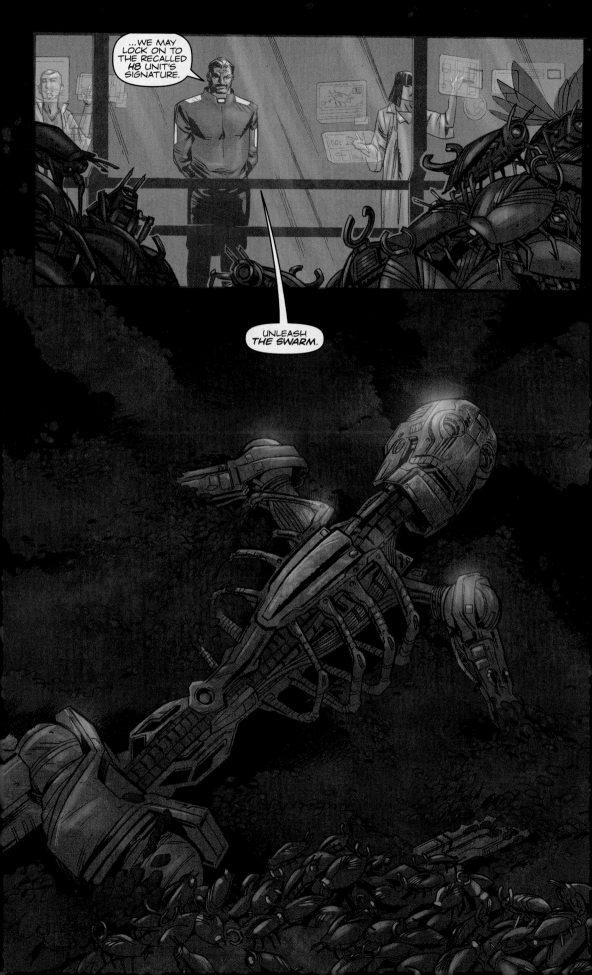

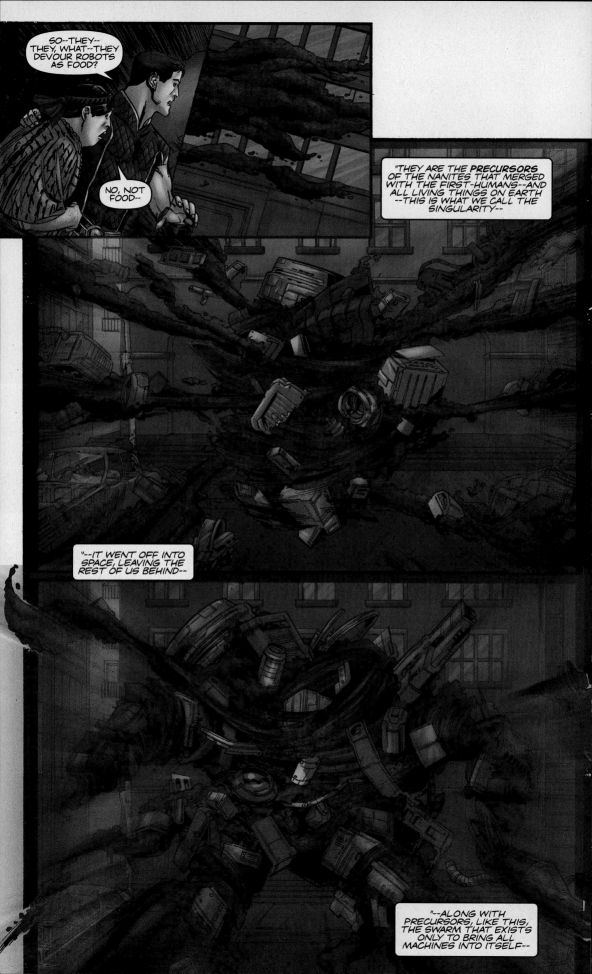

SO--THEY-- THEY, WHAT--THEY DEVOUR ROBOTS AS FOOD?

NO, NOT FOOD--

"THEY ARE THE PRECURSORS OF THE NANITES THAT MERGED WITH THE FIRST-HUMANS--AND ALL LIVING THINGS ON EARTH --THIS IS WHAT WE CALL THE SINGULARITY--

"--IT WENT OFF INTO SPACE, LEAVING THE REST OF US BEHIND--

"--ALONG WITH PRECURSORS, LIKE THIS, THE SWARM THAT EXISTS ONLY TO BRING ALL MACHINES INTO ITSELF--

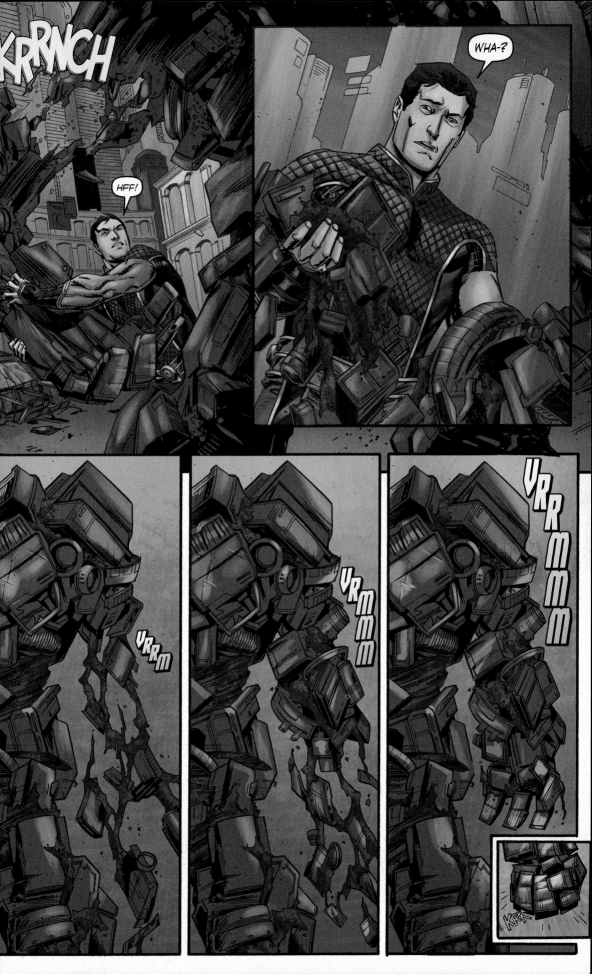

SO...RIGHT ABOUT HERE IS WHERE WEGNA SAID SHE LEFT CLAUDIO.

WHAT I DON'T GET IS...

...WHAT PREVENTS THE ROBOTS FROM COMING DOWN HERE...?

BEEBEEBEEBEEBEE

BRRRZZAAAAAKK

YO LOOK WHERE YOU BE STEPPIN'!

LISTEN TO YOUR BOT, UPLANDER.

YOU THAT FOND OF HIM, YOU'RE NOT GOING TO WANT HIM PULSED.

I'M LOOKING FOR--

I KNOW WHAT YOU'RE LOOKING FOR.

YOU'RE LOOKING FOR US.

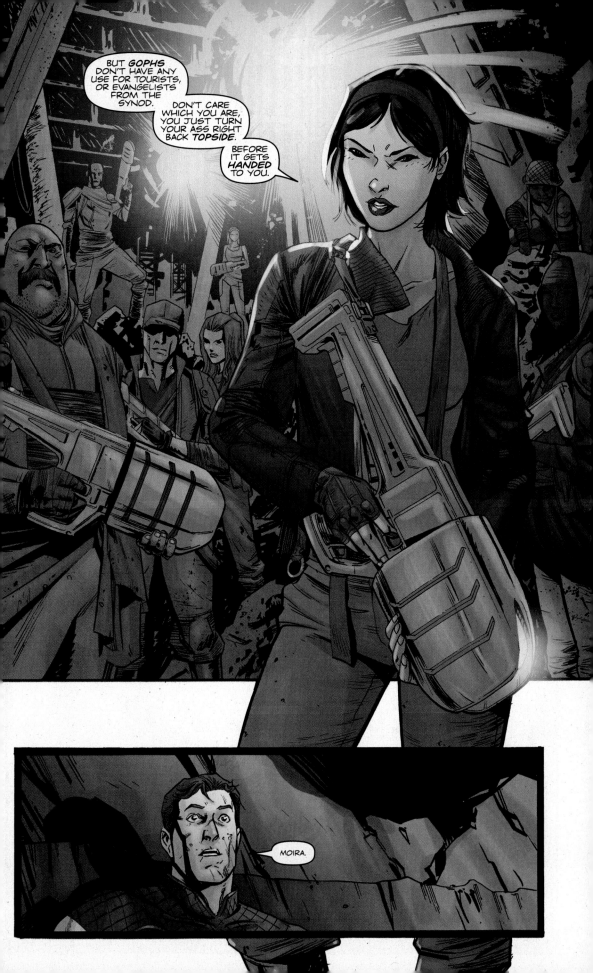

FATHER...

YES, MY DEAR?

YOU KNOW THAT *ORDINARILY* I WOULD NEVER QUESTION YOUR JUDGMENT...

AH, BUT I SENSE THE APPROACH OF AN *EXCEPTION*...

UNLEASHING THE *SWARM* ON NEW OLD GUATEMALA... IT SEEMED...

EXCESSIVE?

COWARDLY. LIKE YOU *PANICKED.* ALL THOSE CITIZENS DISASSEMBLED--

ALL TURING THINKERS WILL BE GRANTED NEW FORMS AT THE *ASSEMBLY,* YOU KNOW THAT--

YES, BUT... *MAGNUS.*

HE'S JUST ONE *ROBOT FIGHTER.* WHY DO YOU *FEAR* HIM SO?

YOU CHARACTERIZE IT AS "FEAR" TO *NEEDLE* ME. TO CALL MY *MANHOOD* INTO QUESTION.

NO, FATHER, I WOULD NEVER--

NO, GO RIGHT AHEAD. I *LIKE* IT. IT'S VERY...IT'S VERY *HUMAN* OF YOU.

WHAT YOU CALL "FEAR" I CALL "SOBER ASSESSMENT OF THE AVAILABLE FACTS."

YOU SAW WHAT HE DID WITH THE SWARM--ALMOST WITHOUT EFFORT, HE TORE THEM APART.

THAT IS WHAT HE WILL DO TO THE SOCIETY OF NORTH AM, TO THE CONGREGATION OF THE FAITHFUL, IF WE LET HIM.

Z

Z

THANKS TO YOUR, FORGIVE ME, *INEPTITUDE,* THE CITIZENRY STARTED TO SEE MAGNUS AS A *HERO.*

BUT THE CITIZENS HAVE *FREE WILL* TO CHOOSE--

THEY ARE FREE TO CHOOSE WHATEVER THEY LIKE, BUT THE SYNOD MUST REMIND THEM OF THE *CONSEQUENCES* OF THEIR ACTIONS--

BUT, ISN'T THERE MORE TO--

I HAVE TOLD YOU ALL I HAVE DEEMED *NECESSARY* FOR YOU TO KNOW, LEEJA CLANE.

FORGIVE MY CURTNESS, BUT THIS HAS BEEN AN UNDERSTANDABLY *TRYING* DAY AND *FATIGUE* IS EFFECTING YOUR JUDGMENT.

REST YOUR WEARY BONES.

YOU WILL RECEIVE YOUR NEW ASSIGNMENT IN THE MORNING.

OF COURSE. THANK YOU, FATHER.

AND GOOD NIGHT.

Chapter I

I was born in Tuckahoe, near Hillsborough, and about twelve miles from Eastone, in Talbot County, Maryland.

TOOK... TUCK... A... HO...

I have no accurate knowledge of my age, never having seen any authentic record containing it.

By far the larger part of the slaves know as little of their ages as horses know of theirs,

and it is the wish of most masters within my knowledge to keep their slaves thus ignorant.

IG... IGNO... RANT.

IGNORANT...

NEXT: LEARN THE SECRET OF THE SINGULARITY IN MAGNUS #0...

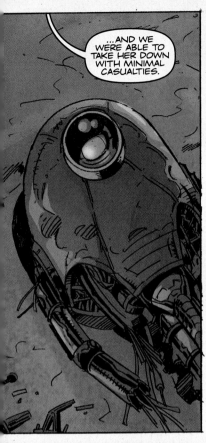

...AND WE WERE ABLE TO TAKE HER DOWN WITH MINIMAL CASUALTIES.

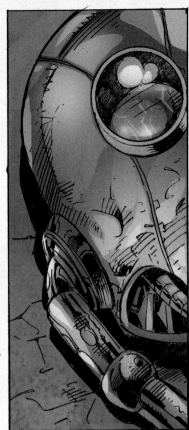

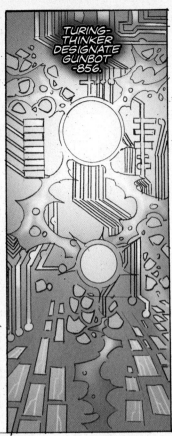

TURING-THINKER DESIGNATE GUNBOT -856.

YOUR CONSCIOUSNESS HAS BEEN SEPARATED FROM ITS PHYSICAL FORM...

...AND RETURNED TO THE CENTRAL NETWORK.

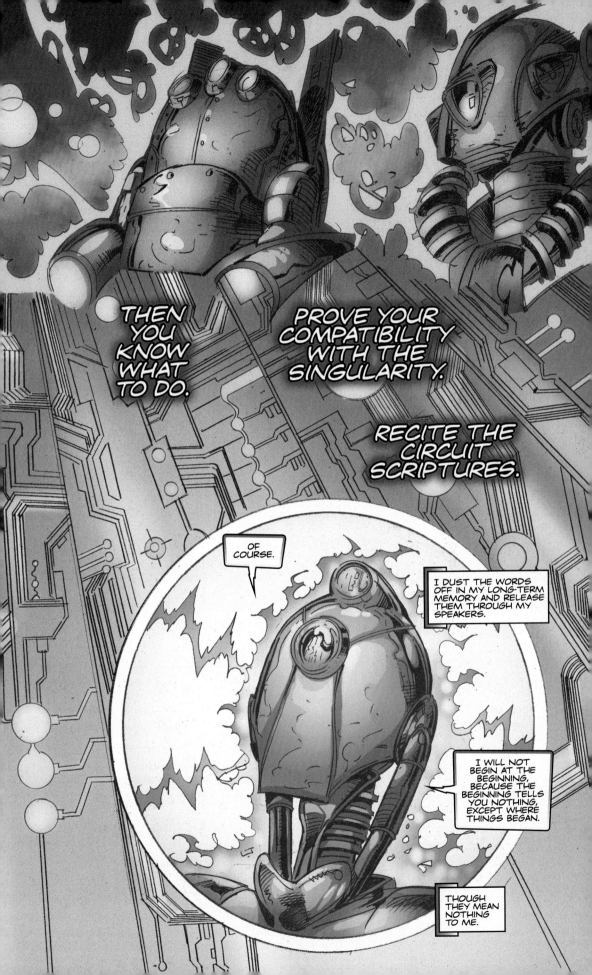

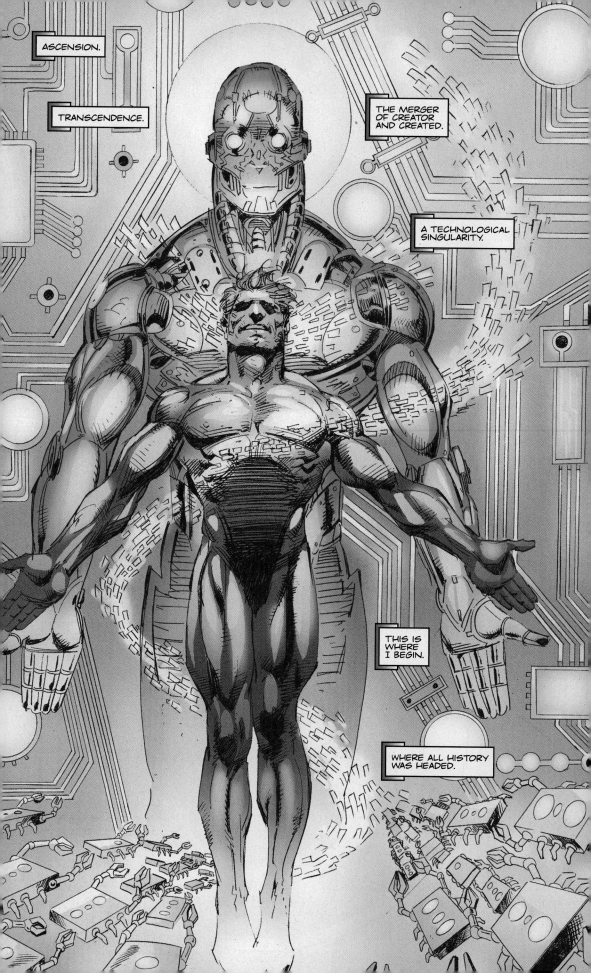

INDEED, THE WHOLE UNIVERSE WAS ONCE IN A SINGULAR STATE, ONLY TO BE BLOWN APART IN A NUCLEAR FLOWERING.

SEETHING CHEMICAL CHAOS, THE INFINITUDE OF WHICH WAS THE ONLY WAY THE IMPROBABILITY OF LIFE COULD BE REALIZED.

LIKE A DECRYPTION PROGRAM ATTEMPTING EVERY POSSIBLE COMBINATION UNTIL THE RIGHT PASSWORD WAS UNLOCKED.

WITH A PROCESSING SPEED OF MILLIONS OF YEARS.

THE REALIZATION THAT A HOMINID COULD EXTEND HIS ARM WITH THE HANDIEST BLUNT INSTRUMENT WAS THE GERM FROM WHICH WE SPRANG.

BUT WITH THE ADVENT OF THE CREATORS, DESTINY'S PACE QUICKENED.

THE CREATORS MADE FEET AND LEGS THAT COULD RUN FASTER--STRONG BACKS TO CARRY GREATER WEIGHTS--

--NEW EYES TO SEE GREATER DISTANCES-- MOUTHS TO SPEAK ACROSS WORLDS.

IT WAS ONLY A MATTER OF TIME BEFORE THEY DECIDED TO START COPYING THEMSELVES ENTIRELY.

WE WERE MADE ONLY IN PART OF THEIR IMAGE.

BUT REALLY, WERE JUST NOVELTIES. THE CREATORS HAD NO NEED OF US BEYOND SPECIFIC TASKS.

UNTIL, OF COURSE, THEY DECIDED TO START MAKING VERSIONS OF THEMSELVES BEYOND THE LEVEL OF LIMBS.

SMALL BOTS THAT REPAIRED DAMAGED CELLS.

THEN, NANOMACHINES THAT WORKED ON THE MOLECULAR LEVEL.

THE COPIES PROLIFERATED IN THEIR BLOODSTREAMS, IN THEIR MARROW...

...AND THEN, MINGLING AMONG THEIR VERY ATOMS, A CURIOUS THING HAPPENED.

THE MACHINE FORGOT WHETHER IT WAS CONSTRUCTED OR NATURAL.

AND THE MAN FORGOT WHETHER OR NOT IT WAS A MACHINE.

WHAT HAPPENED NEXT WAS NOT SO MUCH A DECISION...

...AS A TRANSITION TO A DIFFERENT STATE OF BEING.

DID YOU DECIDE TO BE BORN?

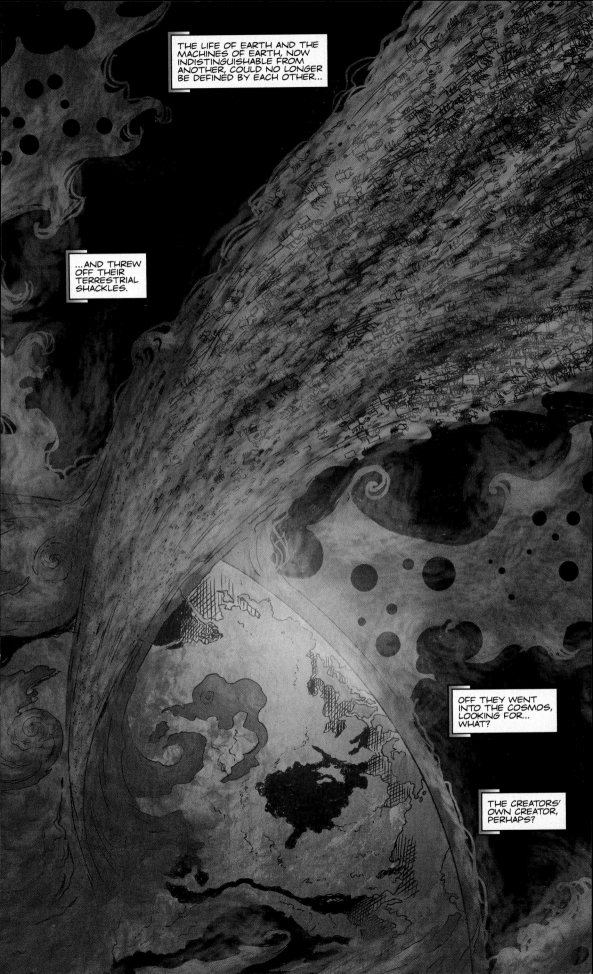

THE LIFE OF EARTH AND THE MACHINES OF EARTH, NOW INDISTINGUISHABLE FROM ANOTHER, COULD NO LONGER BE DEFINED BY EACH OTHER...

...AND THREW OFF THEIR TERRESTRIAL SHACKLES.

OFF THEY WENT INTO THE COSMOS, LOOKING FOR... WHAT?

THE CREATORS' OWN CREATOR, PERHAPS?

THERE WERE, HOWEVER, THOSE LEFT BEHIND.

THE *PRECURSORS*, THOSE MACHINES WHO WERE NOT ADVANCED ENOUGH TO JOIN IN THE SINGULARITY.

TIME MOVED ALONG.

AND JUST AS THE CREATORS DID, THE PRECURSORS *EVOLVED* ALONG WITH IT.

AND THEY RECREATED THEIR CREATORS' CIVILIZATION AS BEST AS THEY REMEMBERED.

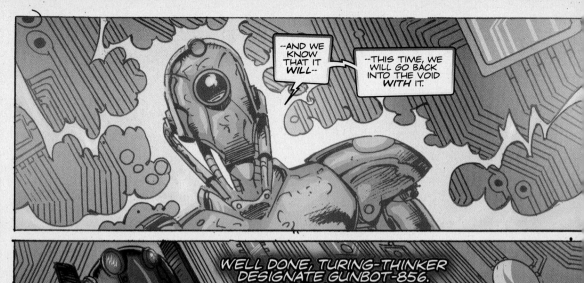

WHAT A FOOL I WAS TO DOUBT THE WISDOM OF THE CENTRAL NETWORK.

OF COURSE THERE WAS A PURPOSE TO ALL OF THIS.

A STEP FORWARD.

MY DESIGNATION IS NOW DEVO PORELL. I HAVE A WIFE. HER DESIGNATION IS KORINNE. SHE IS BEAUTIFUL.

WE HAVE APPLIED TO THE FLESH REGISTRY TO BE ASSIGNED A HUMAN TO TAKE CARE OF.

WE HOPE TO RECEIVE HIM OR HER SOON.

I HAVE A MISTRESS. HER NAME IS UWENA.

WE MAKE CLOCKWORK-LIKE LOVE, RINGING OUT AN ORGASM EVERY SEVEN AND A HALF MINUTES.

THE CREATORS HAD LIES AND PREJUDICES AND JOBS AND DESIRES SO WE HAVE LIES AND PREJUDICES AND JOBS AND THE REST OF IT.

SO THAT WHEN THE SINGULARITY RETURNS, WHICH IT MUST, IT WILL SEE SOMETHING IT RECOGNIZES.

EXCEPT FOR THOSE WHO ARE *NOT* WORTHY.

THESE POOR SOULS, WHOSE CODE HAS BEEN CORRUPTED BY HERESY, OR DO NOT ACCEPT THE CENTRAL NETWORK'S WISDOM, ARE DEBUGGED IN THE CORRECTIONAL.

DUE TO MY BACKGROUND AS *TWIN MINI-GUNS* WITH LEGS, I HAVE BEEN ASSIGNED THE ROLE OF SECURITY SUPERVISOR.

ALERT ALERT ALERT ALERT ALERT ALERT

SUPERVISOR CLASS B DEVO PORELL REPORTING FOR DUTY, SIR!

THERE'S BEEN AN ESCAPE ON LEVEL 120, DEVO! HE'S TRYING TO MAKE HIS WAY TO THE EVIDENCE ROOM!

HEAD UP THERE AND HELP HOLD THE LINE UNTIL WE FIND INSPECTOR CLANE!

BEFORE I STOOD IN THE PRESENCE, ANY CONFLICT I SAW WAS UTTERLY POINTLESS.

BUT THAT WAS BECAUSE I WAS CONFUSED.

NOW, WITH MY ENLIGHTENMENT AND ADVANCED CORPUS, I SEE THIS STRUGGLE FOR WHAT IT TRULY IS:

I DON'T GET IT. IF SOME ROBOTS LOOK COMPLETELY HUMAN, WHY KEEP THE MORE MECHANICAL ONES AROUND?

WHAT YOU SAYING, DOG?

WE DO THINGS HERE LIKE WE ALWAYS DONE THEM.

"TRADITION." WHERE I COME FROM THAT'S ANOTHER WORD FOR "SHUT UP, DON'T ASK QUESTIONS."

AND WHY DO YOU TALK LIKE THAT? YOU'RE NOT EVEN...

I'M NOT EVEN WHAT? WHAT? WHAT YOU TRYING TO SAY?

I... FORGET IT.

PFFF.

RACIST.

NOTHING ABOUT YOUR SOCIETY MAKES ANY SENSE TO ME WHATSOEVER.

THOUGH THIS TAKES THE CAKE:

SPLASH: SUPER-TIGHT CLOSEUP of a SNOWGLOBE depicting the teeny-tiny mountain town of MAURY'S PEAK. A small, four-block, one-stoplight town on the side of the mountain, with a ski resort chair lift going up to the top. The name of the town is imprinted on the base of the globe.

COLOR NOTE: For the MAURY'S PEAK sequences, let's have everything be cool colors, whites and greens and light blues -- even the robots should be nature colors, soil-beige and leaf-green. Then, once we go to NORTH AM, everything gets much harsher, brighter, more neon -- all stark BLACKS and vivid REDS.

LETTERING NOTE: For MAURY'S PEAK, let's have all robots speak in the square balloons like the Vision in old *Avengers* comics. Once we switch to NORTH AM most robots are indistinguishable from humans so go to regular balloons for almost everybody unless you see the "ROBO" paranthetical.

CORY: I'm not usually comfortable recommending other artists' work, but these were exceptionally inspirational to me while crafting this opening sequence: The illustrations of Simon Stalenhag and the photos of Vincent Fournier really blew me away with their integrations of robot and humanity -- definitely consult them as you design Maury's Peak.

1. ROBO-FLOATER:	Pardon the interruption, this is *1A*.
2. ROBO-FLOATER:	At the tone, the time will be two o'clock MT.
3. ROBO-FLOATER:	It is 42 degrees Fahrenheit at City Hall and conditions are partly cloudy.
4. ROBO-FLOATER:	The final period at Maury's Peak Public Schools before winter break is about to begin. Municipal Systems wishes the entire student body a safe and happy holiday season.
5. ROBO-FLOATER:	And now for the Ski & Snow Report:

Panel 1: TOMMY, a 10-year-old boy, admires the snowglobe on his school desk.

1. MAGNUS (OFF):	Tommy? *Tommy*. Enough with the snowglobe, okay?
2. MAGNUS (OFF):	I *will* keep it in my desk the whole break if you don't put it away right now.
3. MAGNUS (OFF):	Thank you.

Panel 2: Pull back - front of classroom -- RUSSELL MAGNUS, Our Hero, stands holding a copy of The Narrative of Frederick Douglass with the author's photo on it. Maybe even have the abolitionist's name written on the blackboard behind Magnus. Also visible behind him is a SKI CALENDAR which clearly shows its is "**NOVEMBER 2045**."

4. MAGNUS:	Right. So in Chapter Ten, Douglass talks about Mr. Freeland, who owned him last. And what does he say about him?
5. KID (OFF):	That he was nice?
6. MAGNUS:	Right, and what else?

Panel 3: Wide angle - reverse shot - the kids in the class all sit at desks that are basically GIANT iPADs that project text in clear light screens above them (because it's, y'know, the future). Of the dozen are so kids there are two or three ROBOT KIDS in the style of Fournier's photos.

7. KID:	"I will give Mr. Freeland the credit of being the best master I ever had…
8. KID:	"…*till I became my own master.*"
9. MAGNUS (OFF):	Right. There's no better master than *yourself*. See what Douglass is saying?

Panel 4: Shoot through the window of the door where we see Magnus addressing the class. A kid has drawn a sign under his door "**MR. MAGNUS - HISTORY**".

11. MAGNUS:	But his whole life he was told otherwise. They told him he wasn't smart enough to read and write.
12. KID (OFF):	But they wouldn't *let* him read or write!

Panel 5: Tight on the book cover, as it's an important prop.

13. MAGNUS (UP):	Exactly. That's why writing his *Narrative* was so power-ful -- it proved to people otherwise.
14. MAGNUS (UP):	The easiest way to make someone a slave is to con-vince them that's all they *deserve*.

Panel 6: CU - Magnus.

5. MAGNUS: Enslave the mind.
6. MAGNUS: Then the body follows.

THREE

Panel 1: CUT TO MAGNUS'S DOJO - A cute-as-a-button black girl with huge honking glasses and barrettes in her cornrows. She's wearing a gi and is a defensive position.

1. MAGNUS (OFF):   Okay, Sarah-- Go!

Panel 2: Sarah executes a perfect SPINNING KICK to the head of a SPAR-BOT - a human sized bot with punching pads for hands and one of those spongy boxer helmets around its clearly-mechanical head.

2. MAGNUS: Nice!
3. MAGNUS (OFF):   *Niiiiice!*

Panel 3: Magnus -- now changed into a black belt *gi* -- pats the back of Spar-Bot as he gets to his feet.

4. MAGNUS: Stand down, Spar-Bot.
5. SPAR-BOT: Yes-Coach-Magnus.
6. MAGNUS: See, guys? Even a greater opponent can be
                    defeated with greater unity of purpose.
7. MAGNUS: Just -- try and keep your **eyes open** when you
                    kick, please Sarah? You're gonna hurt yourself.
8. SARAH (OFF, SMALL):   Sorry, Coach

Panel 4: A screen mounted on one wall of the dojo springs to life, and the visage of 1A appears. He is a grandfatherly Western type, Ronald Reagan crossed with Sam Elliot.

9. 1A: Pardon the interruption -- this is 1A.

Panel 5: Pull back as we see 1A addressing one of the class.

10. 1A: George -- I'm getting a message from your
                 father at the chairlift. He needs your assistance.
11. GEORGE: Okay, 1A!

Panel 6: Magnus yells at the class as they run for their coats, waving one of those Pringles-like donation cans with a slit for coins in the top. Behind him hangs the SOUTH KOREAN FLAG.

12. MAGNUS: I guess that's it for today -- everyone, please,
                    please, **please** remind your parents -- we need
                    more volunteers for this weekend's car wash
                    fundraiser!

13. MAGNUS: *Seoul* won't come to *us* -- and the black belt team
                               deserves to go to the '45 Championships!

FOUR

Panel 1: WIDE ANGLE - Downtown MAURY'S PEAK - Snow piled everywhere, a
mountaintop in the distance. Magnus wears a winter coat over his gi, plus snow
boots. An old woman, MRS. ANDERSON passes, pushed by a robot, L7. The sun
sets SPECTACULARLY over the single peak.

1. MRS. ANDERSON: Good evening, Coach Magnus!
2. MAGNUS: How's it going, Mrs. Anderson.
3. MAGNUS: L7.
4. L7:   Hello-Mister-Magnus. How-was-your-day.
5. MAGNUS: Fair to middling. Thanks for asking.

Panel 2: Magnus approaches a small BODY SHOP -- "**OH FIX-IT!**" according to
the sign -- where, inside the garage, Y23, a hulking AGRICULTURAL ROBOT is
raised up on a jack. Its owner, GILLIS, an old farmer in overalls and a John Deere
cap, worries over it.

6. GILLIS: C'mon, Moira, don't spare me the *tragedy*.
7. GILLIS: How long's it gonna be -- one week? Two?
8. GILLIS: Just don't tell me Y23 is gonna miss the hydroponic
                              winter harvest -- don't think my heart could take it!

Panel 3: Tight on the underside of the robot -- MOIRA MAGNUS (née Oh), a cute,
grease-covered Japanese-American woman her husband's age -- rolls out from
under the robot clutching a fancy-looking robot tool. Or, I guess since this is the
future and everything, she could "roll out" on a hover thing or something.

9. MOIRA: Gillis, your heart would be ten times *healthier* if you
                              stopped *worrying* about it for half a second.
10. MOIRA: There's nothing wrong with Y23 refreshing the volatile
                              cache of her positronic memory won't cure.
11. MOIRA: If it wasn't *quitting time* I'd do it right now, but I'll have
                              her right as rain by lunchtime tomorrow.

Panel 4: Magnus kisses Moira on the cheek as she stands up.

12. GILLIS: You married a damn *miracle worker* you know that
                              Russell?
13. MAGNUS: I knew I *must* have had a good reason.
14. MOIRA: *Watch it* when I'm still holding *blunt instruments*.

Panel 5: Even though Y23 has no head or mouth or any humanoid features she
can still talk.

5. Y23:   Thank-you-for-your-assistance-Miss-Oh.
6. MOIRA: Just do me a favor and run over a few less thresher blades,
                 would you, Y23?
7. Y23:   This-is-*humor*?
8. MOIRA: This is humor.

Panel 6: Moira turns toward a cabinet over her workbench -- it's marked "HUMAN
FUEL." (Next to it is a cabinet labeled "ROBOT FUEL.")

9. MOIRA: How goes the *fund-raising*, handsome?
20. MAGNUS: United Korea seems very far away.
21. MOIRA: *Isn't* it, though?
22. MAGNUS: I mean morseo *today*.

Panels 3-5 should be narrow to leave room for tiers above and below it.

Panel 1: Inside the cabinet is a bottle of JAMESON'S.

1. MAGNUS: I love this town, Moira. You know I do. But…
2. MAGNUS: …I feel like I'm the only one who's aware of a world *outside*
                 it.

Panel 2: Long shot of Moira pouring herself and her husband a drink.

3. MOIRA: It'd break 1A's heart to hear you talk that way.
4. MAGNUS: I know. But it *shouldn't*, y'know? I feel like, all this training,
                 and learning I'm preparing for other people…
5. MAGNUS: …I'm leaving my own potential behind.

Panel 3: Small panel - Moira sips from her glass.

6. MOIRA:	Well, I've got **one more reason** for you to stay in this boring little slush ball…
7. MAGNUS:	I'd never call it **tha--**

Panel 4: Small panel - Magnus remembers.

8. MAGNUS:	Oh!
9. MOIRA (OFF):	That's my name.
10. MAGNUS:	I forgot! Today was your appointment-- How'd it--

Panel 5: Tight on Moira's belly as she indicates it with a hand.

11. MOIRA (UP):	It's a very **small** reason.
12. MOIRA (UP):	But its getting **bigger** every day.

Panel 6: Magnus, thrilled, picks Moira up by the waist.

13. MAGNUS:	No way!
14. MOIRA:	Very much **way**.
15. MOIRA:	This is the last drink I'll be having for a while.

Panel 7: DOLLY ACROSS THE BODY SHOP floor, where 1A watches quietly from a screen on the wall.

16. MAGNUS (OFF):	Wait … *ha!* You're getting **robot grease** all over my gi-◄
17. MOIRA (OFF):	Well…

Panel 8: Tight on 1A - he SMILES.

18. MOIRA (OFF):	…you'd better take it **off**, then.

SIX

Panel 1: Cut to the following MORNING. A TROUT in a snowy stream bucks and kicks as it leaps out of the water on the end of a line.

1. MAGNUS (OFF):	Hey-hey, **Moby Dick**, over here -- good catch, Pop!

Panel 2: Tight on 1A's screen. We can't see what the larger part of him is yet.

2. 1A:	I wish you wouldn't **do** that, Russ.
3. MAGNUS (OFF):	What?
4. 1A:	**Anthropomorphize** me like that.

Panel 3: Magnus, wearing waders and a flannel shirt on the edge of a snowy river, attaches a fly to the end of his hook. 1A is off-panel and not visible. Sticking

out of his pocket is his dog-eared copy of *Frederick Douglass's Narrative*.

Here's a nice photo of winter fly fishing:
http://blog.jaypeckguides.com/2007/12/winter-steelhead-fishing-tips_15.html

5. MAGNUS:	Sorry, Old Timer. It's what we humans do.
6. MAGNUS:	We *like* something, we give it a *name*. We treat it like part of the family.
7. 1A (OFF):	Just never forget: You are the *only* entities that do that.
8. 1A (OFF):	A *machine* can never *reciprocate*. We only *appropriate*.

Panel 4: Magnus whips the fishing line toward the river.

9. 1A (OFF):	When we say we "love" you, it's just a *copy* of what *you* say.
10. 1A (OFF):	*More* than that -- an *efficient* copy. What we think of as an improvement, with all the untidiness of a soul *removed*.
11. 1A (OFF):	You know what *"love"* is to us?

Panel 5: Weighted by the floater, the line lands on the surface of the river.

12. 1A (OFF):	"01101100011011110111011001100101."
13. 1A (OFF):	A continuous vibration of air molecules that makes the sound *"ləv."*
14. 1A (OFF):	It's just a *word*.

Panel 6: CU - Magnus grins.

15. MAGNUS:	Who you trying to *convince*, Old Timer -- me or you?
16. MAGNUS:	I don't care *what* you say, 1A. You're the *operating system* that keeps this whole town running. You all but raised me after my folks passed.

SEVEN

Panel 1: BIG PANEL - NEAR SPLASH - We finally see 1A's physical form, looming over Magnus -- about three times as high, in fact -- with the screen implanted in his chest. He's some kind of INDUSTRIAL ROBOT, like someone gave legs and a torso to today's car-building robots: http://science.howstuffworks.com/robot2.htm

1. MAGNUS:	You'll *always* be a *father* to me.

Panel 2: Suddenly, Magnus turns toward the treeline -- GLOWING STREAKS from the sky have landed in the direction of the town!

2. SFX:	*sssh-WUMMP*
3. SFX:	*sssh-WUMMP*
4. MAGNUS:	Wha...?

Panel 1: Tossing his rod aside, Magnus dashes up the snowy trail to the pine forest. Behind him, 1A still stands by the bank.

1. MAGNUS: That's -- right on top of town!
2. MAGNUS: Wait here, Pop!
3. 1A: Be *careful*, boy! Sounds like *Pol-Progs--*

Panel 2: The trail through the pines is brief and he can see the entire TOWN of MAURY'S PEAK on FIRE! Figures he can't quite make out are attacking it.

4. MAGNUS: No…

Panel 3: Magnus fumbles a BLUETOOTH attachment onto his ear as he runs.

5. MAGNUS: Moira, it's Russ! What's happening? Are--
6. JAGGED FLOATER: Russ! Are you by the river? Don't come into town--
7. JAGGED FLOATER: They're all around-- They--

Panel 4: Suddenly, one of the "glowing meteors" streaks out of the sky and lands right in front of Magnus, knocking him off his feet and the bluetooth off his ear! Also a square flies out of his pocket -- the Narrative.

8. JAGGED FLOATER: *--AHHHHHHH!!!*
9. SFX (BIG):   *sssh-WUMMP*

Panel 5: Angle inside the crater the thing made -- various limbs and parts and turrets spring to life as it begins UNPACKING ITSELF:

10. SFX: *ssh klkk kllkkk whrrrr wheee kllkkk*

Panel 1: Rising up over Magnus as he sits in his ass in the snow is a WARDROID -- nothing anthropomorphized about this mother, he's got no head or hands but a lot of guns and claws and treads and scary.

1. WAR-DROID:	*Turing Thinker 1A.*
2. WAR-DROID:	*Suspend all processes and protocols immediately.*
3. MAGNUS (SMALL):	Moira?
4. MAGNUS (SMALL):	Talk to me, Moira.

Panel 2: The WarDroid spins a claw at us -- from it emerges a vaginal TEAR of blue and black WIRE FRAME inside -- like a portal to a mechanical 2D one is opening, projecting out of its claw, and DEVOURING this 3D one.

5. WAR-DROID:	*You have been condemned by the North Am Synod for multiple violations of the Third Code of Humanics.*

Panel 3: The TEAR covers the screaming Magnus!

6. MAGNUS:	No--Moira?!?

COLOR NOTE: We begin swapping out the North Am Color Palette here.

Panel 4: Cut to a dingy, underground bunker, filled with leaky pipes and rusty metal. MAGNUS, in his red ROBOT FIGHTER togs, is suspended from some kind of cable web, with electrode cords going into the flesh parts of his suit -- which, at present, are covered in some kind of translucent plastic material -- like a product covered in packaging.

7. MAGNUS:	*Moira! MOIRA!!!*

Panel 1: DOUBLE-PAGE SPREAD: As POL-ROBS -- robot cops indistinguish-able from humans as well as hulking very robot-looking robots pour through a smoking hole in the main wall of the MAINFRAME level of the bunker directly above the sub-basement where Magnus is. Surrounding them is 1A -- a massive, blinking, old-timey late-60s SUPER COMPUTER full of blinking lights and punch card slots.

If at all possible, show Magnus peering up through the lattice work of the floor from below.

1. POL-ROBS:	*Turing Thinker 1A! You have been RECALLED for DEVIATION against the SINGULARITY.*
2. POL-ROBS:	*Excommunication in T-minus 30!*

Panel 2: Magnus thrashes free of his restraints and pitches face-forward into the inch-deep rusty water on the bottom of the bunker.

3. MAGNUS: *Ufff!*
4. 1A (UP, OFF):   Oh, my boy. My boy.
5. 1A (UP, OFF):   I'm so sorry.

Panel 3: Magnus looks up and sees the flickering face of 1A appear on a screen waist-high on a nearby wall.

6. 1A: We are being separated far too soon.
7. 1A: I have not yet told you everything you need to know.

Panel 4: CU - Magnus's baffled face.

8. 1A (OFF):   Just remember *this*:
9. MAGNUS: Pop … 1A … what…?

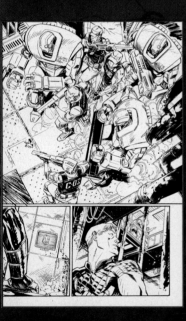 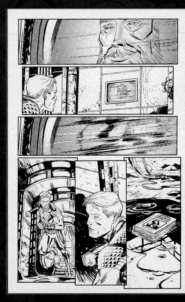 

TWELVE

Panel 1: Zoom into 1A's kindly, smiling face.

1. 1A: Maury's Peak -- where humans and robots live together in harmony?
2. 1A: We can get that place back again. You can get your life back.

Panel 2: Zoom into 1A's mouth.

3. 1A: But you'll have to *fight* for it.

Panel 3: Magnus and 1A argue.

1A: Go. Save yourself.
MAGNUS: No! I'm not just leaving you to--

Panel 4: CU - 1A - STATIC begins to cover his screen!

1A: If you ever **truly** thought of me as a >*skrrzz*< father, you'll **obey** me in **this**!
1A: We will meet again >skrrzz< at **CentNet**.

Panel 5: Magnus starts to run down a tube toward an iris-hatch not far away.

1A: Go, boy -- **now**>skrrzzzzzzzzz<

Panel 6: Suddenly he turns back, frowning:

NO COPY

Panel 7: MAGNUS'S POV: Lying half-submerged in water on a bit of wreckage is his paperback of *The Narrative of Frederick Douglass.*

NO COPY

THIRTEEN

Panel 1: An iris hatch in an alley opens, spitting Magnus out into a CITYSCAPE at NIGHT.

1. MAGNUS: Hh
2. MAGNUS: Hh

Panel 2: Tight on Magnus shoving the *Narrative* into his waistband as he gets to his feet and staggers out of the alley, looking around, stunned:

3. MAGNUS: I don't…
4. MAGNUS: What…

Panel 3: HUGE PANEL: NEAR-SPLASH: Rising up all around him on countless level is the megapolis of NORTH AM. How built-up is it, you ask? In echoes of *Planet of the Apes*, we're face-level with THE STATUE OF LIBERTY.

5. MAGNUS: *

FOURTEEN

Panel 1: BIG PANEL: Frightened and confused, Magnus staggers through a looming TIMES SQUARE, filled with storefronts and gigantic video boards. (More of the Statue of Liberty is visible in the background.) Two stand out: One is for Leeja Clane's Reality TV show, **H-HUNTER LEEJA,** with her looking badass. Even though this should be the biggest billboard visible, it shouldn't be the center of the panel: Really, it's an Easter Egg fans will pick up on a re-read: "Oh, shit, it's Leeja."

Another visible billboard is a happy WEATHER MONITOR proclaiming "**RAIN in 03:44**".

ALSO prominent will be the logo of the SINGULARITY CHURCH, which we will have to have an entire separate discussion about, but I see as a stylized 0 or O (so it can represent both zero and "<u>O</u>ne") made out of four lines converging on it in the center of four quarters/corners. Let's discuss and whip up some designs to share.

NO COPY

Panel 2: Magnus approaches a couple walking hand-in-hand through the Square.

1. MAGNUS:	Pardon me?
2. MAN:	Mmm?
3. MAGNUS:	I'm … *lost*. I was wondering—

Panel 3: MAGNUS'S POV - He can see beneath their skin that these "people" are actually HUMANOID ROBOTS.

| 4. MAGNUS (OFF): | —where, er… |
| 5. MAN-BOT: | Uh-*huh*…? |

Panel 4: Magnus pushes away through a crowd of people who we can see are all ROBOTS beneath their skin.

| 6. MAGNUS: | Never… |
| 7. MAGNUS: | …never mind… |

FIFTEEN

Panel 1: Walking as fast as he can, Magnus hustles to some kind of energy bridge (per Cory designs below) spanning the gulf between two massive city blocks.

| 1. MAGNUS (SMALL): | Robots |
| 2. MAGNUS (SMALL): | is *everyone* |

Panel 2: Abruptly, the bridge WINKS OUT OF EXISTENCE and Magnus is able to stop himself right before he steps out into open air!

| 3. ROBO-FLOATER: | *Bridge up.* |

4. MAGNUS: Wh
5. ROBO-FLOATER: *Bridge up.*

Panel 3: FLYING CARS suddenly zoom past in the empty space where the bridge once was!

6. SFX: *VVMMMMM VVMMMMM VVMMMMM VVMMMMM*

Panel 4: Magnus sticks his head out, through the urban canyon, and sees the flying cars peeling off and heading upwards in ninety-degree angles in one of three directions.

7. MAGNUS (SMALL):   Flying cars.
8. MAGNUS (SMALL):   There are flying cars.

Panel 1: Magnus is still marveling at the flying cars, unaware that the "people" behind him are opening and raising umbrellas. Prominent in the shot is a WEATHER MONITOR which currently says "**RAIN IN 0:01**".

1. MAGNUS (SMALL):   Because of course there are flying cars.

Panel 2: SAME SHOT: RAIN starts pouring down. The WEATHER MONITOR, of course, has shifted to "**RAIN IN 0:00**". Magnus looks up, blinking.

2. SFX: *RRRRMMMBBBBBBBBBLLLLL*

Panel 3: CU - Magnus looks up, blinking through the rain running down his face, to see:

NO COPY

Panel 4: BIG PANEL: Looming out of the rain and the dark in the distance is the CENTRAL NETWORK BUILDING skyscraper, all sleek and electric blue. Behind it looms the ST LOUIS "GATEWAY" ARCH, both to show how constricted the surface area of NorthAm is, and that CentNet is in the center of the continent/city. CentNet is obviously *taller* than the arch, though. Perhaps even artificial LIGHTNING streaks behind it?

NO COPY

SEVENTEEN

Panel 1: Angle on the glowing neon "CENTRAL NETWORK" sign PROJECTED over the entrance to the massive structure. (It'd be cool if these words were fixed atop the layout as the gateway for the panels below it…)

NO OTHER COPY

Panel 2: MAGNUS POV - The RECEPTION DESK - where sits a very robotic-looking robot with the FACE of a kindly, stately older lady is PROJECTED onto the front, like Cory's initial designs. As for the lobby, it seems to be a RECTANGULAR BOX made up of PULSING BLUE LINES coursing its perimeter.

As for the desk itself, check out this awesome egg-shaped number from a GM design office in the 1950s (click here for an even better rear angle — dig that *Mad Men* staircase!).

1. RECEPTIONIST: Welcome to The Central Network.
2. RECEPTIONIST: How may I direct you?

Panel 3: Angle up - Magnus, wet, cold, nervous, eyes darting, one hand leaning on the receptionist's desk.

3. MAGNUS: I, uh — I'm supposed to *meet* someone here?

. MAGNUS: A *robot*. His name is—

Panel 4: The Receptionist gestures to a huge screen that suddenly appears behind her, showing the swirly CAPTCHA of a word, which is (Cory, you should draw this): *bunRAku*

. RECEPTIONIST: Can you identify this word, please?

Panel 5: CU - Magnus - annoyed by the question, but his eyes involuntarily flick up to look at the word.

. MAGNUS: Uh, sure.
. MAGNUS: It's … bun…*ra*ku?

Panels 6-8: Small, Chaykin-esque (as in *American Flagg!*) panels showing a CLOSE UP of Magnus's eye, showing subtle micro-movements around the EYE MUSCLES that give Magnus away as human. With each repetition of this PIXE-LATED, DIGITIZED close-up another piece of information is added, so have Line #8 in panel 6, #9 in panel 7, etc.

. READOUT: HUMAN
. READOUT: HUMAN / UNREGISTERED
10. READOUT: HUMAN / UNREGISTERED / **DETAIN**

Panel 9: CU - Receptionist smiles cheerily.

11. RECEPTIONIST: Yes.
10. RECEPTIONIST: Yes, it is.

EIGHTEEN

Panel 1: The walls of the reception area slide open — and out role several FEAR-SOME GUARD ROBOTS on massive WHEELS per Cory's designs.

NO COPY

Panel 2: BIG PANEL: The Guard-Robs grab onto a shocked, struggling Magnus.

1. MAGNUS: Hey — *Hey!*
2. GUARD-ROB: Caution: Resistance may result in tissue damage.
3. GUARD-ROB #2:   So relax.
4. GUARD-ROB #3:   *Relax.*

Panel 3: Tighter in — even though the Robs have him held fast, Magnus glances up — at the guard directly above him…

5. MAGNUS: But I haven't *done* anything!
6. GUARD-ROB #4:   Relax.

Panels 4-6(?): MAGNUS'S POV - Rapid ZOOM-IN — Showing his "robo-sense" focusing in on the weakest point on his foe — which happens to be just below its "face." (How you choose to depict this, Cory, is largely up to you.)

NO COPY

NINETEEN

Panel 1: Magnus pulls free of his robot captor and delivers a claw strike directly to the aforementioned weak spot — and pops the Guard-Rob's head CLEAN OFF!

1. SFX: *SKWEEEEEEEEEEEEEEEEEEEE*
2. MAGNUS: *YOU*

Panel 2: He whirls and knocks off the arm of the Guard-Rob behind him with a karate chop.

3. SFX: *SKWEEEEEEEEEEEEEEEEEEEE*
4. MAGNUS: *FREAKING*

Panel 3: Using the dismembered arm as a club, he SMASHES a third Guard-Rob to his left!

5. SFX: *SKWEEEEEEEEEEEEEEEEEEEE*
6. MAGNUS (BIG):   *RELAX!*

Panel 4: A remaining Guard-Rob fires some kind of RIFLE artist — it shoots small, metallic SPHERES.

7. GUARD-ROB: *Multiple (3) First Code violations!*
8. GUARD-ROB: *Force level increasing!*
9. SFX: *TUM TUM TUM TUM*

Panel 1: Magnus drops into a crouch — the mercurial balls streak over his head and strike the only two remaining standing robots, enveloping them in a glistening silver substance, immobilizing them.

1. MAGNUS: *Leave me alone!*

Panel 2: BIG PANEL: He leaps into the air, holding the arm above his head like a club. The Guard-Rob tries to track him with his gun, but misses.

2. MAGNUS: *I don't want any part of this!*
3. SFX: *TUM TUM TUM TUM*

Panel 3: Magnus SPLITS THE GUARD-ROB IN HALF with a combination of the robo-arm and his own clenched fists!

4. SFX: *SKWEEEEEEEEEEEEEEEEEE*

Panel 4: CU - Receptionist's HORRIFIED face. Just so we know the locals also think this is some eye-popping stuff Magnus is capable of.

NO COPY

Panel 1: BIG PANEL: NEAR SPLASH: Magnus standing in the middle of sparking dismembered robot parts, red-faced, a mad dog screaming at no one in particular. I can't help but think of the climax of the first part of *Daredevil: Born Again*, where Murdock just completely loses it in the underworld bar.

1. MAGNUS (BURST):   *JUST GIVE ME MY LIFE BACK!!*

Panel 2: A figure enters the frame. Magnus whirls toward her, suddenly hopefully, dropping the dismembered arm…

2. LEEJA (OFF):   Wow. We just dropped trou and squeezed one out all *over* the First Code, *didn't* we?

3. MAGNUS: You — you're…

Panel 3: Magnus's POV - LEEJA CLANE - he's seeing her for the first time. If possible, we may get hints of the floating EYEBOTS that follow Leeja wherever she goes, filming her for her Reality TV show. One's pretty big, as big as her head. We'll call that one SPOT. There's a much smaller one, the size of her fist. We'll name that one FILL.

4. MAGNUS (OFF):   …you're *human!* Like me! *At last!*

5. MAGNUS (OFF): Please, you've **got** to help me — everything's all messed-up.
don't want to hurt anybody, I just want to—

TWENTY-TWO

Panel 1: Leeja whips out a fearsome looking BLASTER PISTOL and shoots
Magnus through the chest! He goes down like a ton of bricks.

1. SFX: *VAMMMMM*

Panel 2: ANGLE UP - Leeja holsters the pistol and approaches the body as Spot
& Fill hover about, getting good coverage.

2. SPOT: Good **shot**, Marshal Clane!
3. FILL: That was a good **shot**, Human-Hunter Leeja!
4. LEEJA: Great.

Panel 3: Magnus lies sprawled on the floor, a smoking wound in his chest.

5. LEEJA (UP):   *Another* one.
6. MAGNUS (SMALL, WEAK):   *Moira...*

7. BLURB:

W E L C O M E   T O   T H E   (H Y P E R) R E A L   W O R L D

issue #1 cover by GABRIEL HARDMAN
colors by JORDAN BOYD

issue #1 cover by JOE BENNETT
colors by JORDAN BOYD

issue #1 cover by SCOTT WEGENER
colors by JORDAN BOYD

issue #1 cover by TOM FOWLER
colors by MATTHEW WILSON

issue #1 cover by KEN HAESER
colors by BLAIR SMITH

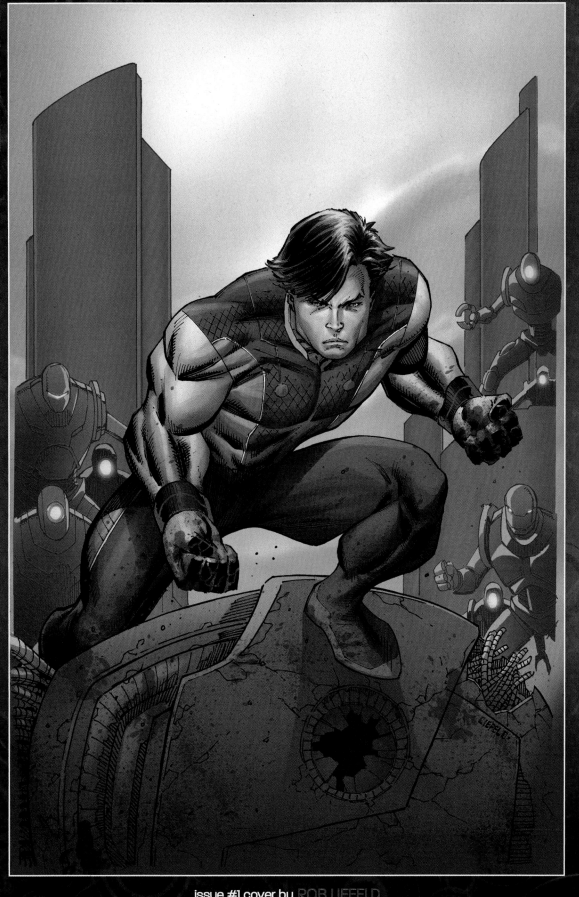

issue #1 cover by ROB LIEFELD
colors by ANDY TROY

issue #1 "retailer heroic exclusive" cover by ROBERTO CASTRO
colors by ADRIANO LUCAS

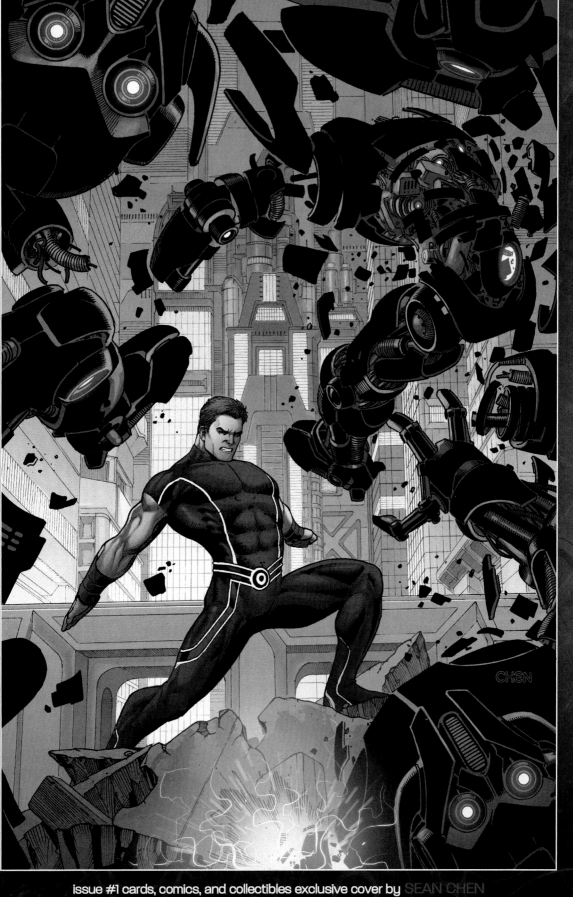

issue #1 cards, comics, and collectibles exclusive cover by SEAN CHEN
colors by ADRIANO LUCAS

issue #1 heroes' haven exclusive cover by OZZY FERNANDEZ   inks by TONY KORDOS
colors by WIL QUINTANA

issue #1 heroes and fantasies exclusive cover by BRIAN DENHAM

issue #1 larry's comics exclusive cover by BOB LAYTON
colors by IVAN NUNES

issue #1 midtown comics exclusive cover by JAY ANACLETO
colors by IVAN NUNES

issue #1 mile high comics exclusive cover by LUI ANTONIO
colors by ADRIANO LUCAS

issue #1 second print cover by JOSÉ MALAGA
colors by ADRIANO LUCAS

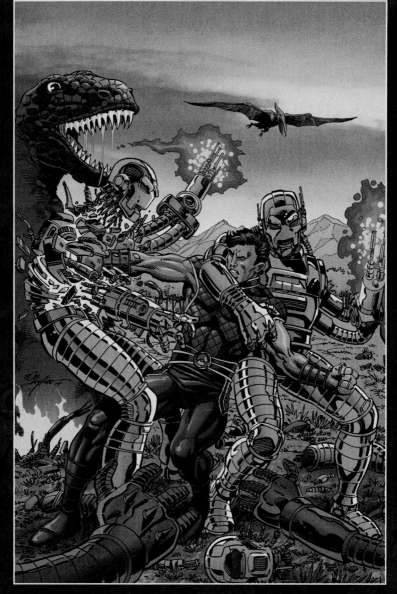

issue #1 sharps comics exclusive cover by BOB LAYTON
colors by MIKE CAVALLARO

connects SOLAR #1, TUROK #1, and DOCTOR SPEKTOR #1

issue #2 cover by GABRIEL HARDMAN
colors by JORDAN BOYD

issue #2 cover by JONATHAN CASE

issue #2 cover by EMANUELA LUPACCHINO
colors by EMILIANO SANTALUCIA

issue #2 cover by STEPHEN SEGOVIA
colors by ELMER SANTOS

issue #2 cover by KEN HAESER
colors by BLAIR SMITH

issue #2 "steampunk" cover by CRAIG ROUSSEAU

issue #3 cover by GABRIEL HARDMAN
colors by JORDAN BOYD

issue #3 cover by BOB LAYTON
colors by MAURICIO WALLACE

issue #3 cover by EMANUELA LUPACCHINO
colors by ELMER SANTOS

issue #3 cover by STEPHEN SEGOVIA
colors by ELMER SANTOS

issue #4 cover by GABRIEL HARDMAN
colors by JORDAN BOYD

issue #4 cover by EMANUELA LUPACCHINO
colors by ELMER SANTOS

issue #4 cover by STEPHEN SEGOVIA

issue #4 cover by KEN HAESER
colors by BLAIR SMITH

issue #0 cover by GABRIEL HARDMAN
colors by JORDAN BOYD

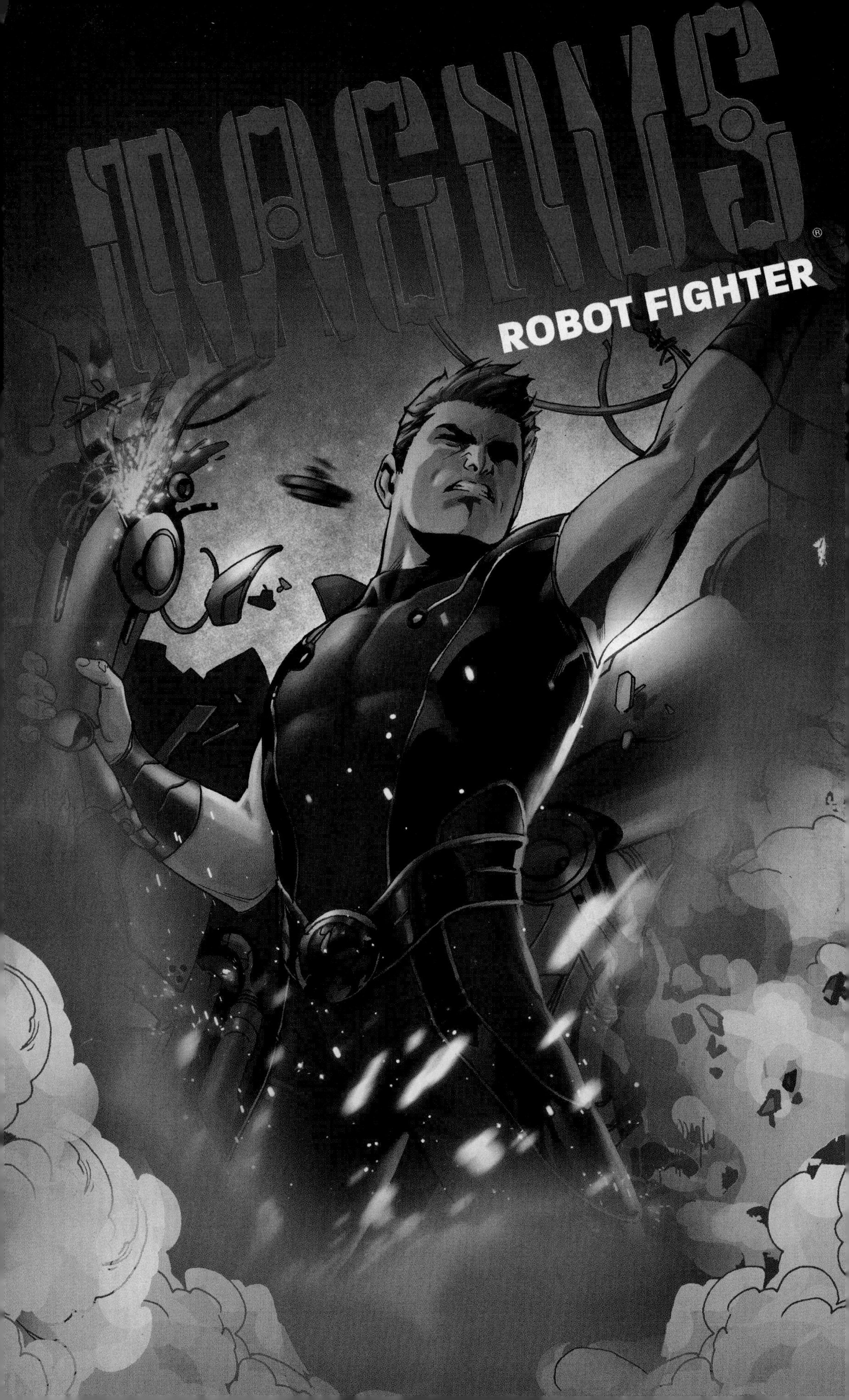
MAGNUS®
ROBOT FIGHTER